Disaster at the Dardanelles, 1915

Edwin P. Hoyt

Disaster at the Dardanelles, 1915

Arthur Barker Limited
London
A subsidiary of Weidenfeld (Publishers) Limited

Contents

Notes

In the preparation of this book I used a large and varied list of sources, from the naval museum at Greenwich to the Public Records Office, which has all the original records tucked away. At the latter, the most interesting and poignant document pertaining to the Dardanelles adventure was the report on the plan of attack submitted by Vice-Admiral Carden at the request of the Admiralty with an enthusiastic marginal comment and the magic initials wsc.

Basic to the study is Sir Julian Corbett's history of naval operations in the First World War, and perhaps equally important here Brigadier General C.F. Aspinall-Oglander's *Military Operations Gallipoli*, a part of the official *History of the Great War*. I used it thoroughly and found it invaluable. Winston S. Churchill's *The World Crisis* was important, particularly the volume on 1915, which tells much of Churchill's activity and thinking of the period. The Navy Records Society's Keyes Papers were also important, to show an operational point of view.

At the Public Records Office, the reports of Vice-Admiral Carden and de Robeck were valuable, as were the logs and records of the various ships and commands which participated in the action. At the Imperial War Museum I consulted Chrisman's *Naval Operations in the Mediterranean;* Wester-Wemyss's *The Navy in the Dardanelles Campaign*; Woodward's *The Escape of the Goeben and Breslau, August 1914;* Edwin Gray's *A Damned Un-English Weapon*; Chack's *Sur Mer et Dessous*; E.K. Chatterton's *Dardanelles Dilemma*; K. Edwards' *We Dive at Dawn;* H. W. Nevinson's *The Dardanelles Campaign*; and Dr Oscar Parkes's *British Battleships*.

At various times, at Greenwich, at the British Museum, at the Navy Museum in London, I consulted many other works and discussed the Dardanelles with various officers. C.E. Caldwell's *The Dardanelles* was valuable, as were E. Dane's *British Campaigns in the Nearer East* and De Loghe's *The Straits Impregnable* and, of course, Parliament's Dardanelles Commission Report, which has in its own voluminous way the complete record of everything that happened and nearly everything that anyone thought about it at the time.

Edwin P. Hoyt

1 Escape of
Goeben and *Breslau*

On the day that a wild-eyed radical pulled out a weapon and assassinated the Archduke Franz Ferdinand of Austro-Hungary in the dusty street of Sarajevo, all countries of western and eastern Europe began to look to their defences. Depending to some extent on the conduct of Italy in the coming months, Britain and France thought they would not have too difficult a time keeping the Mediterranean an Allied sea. The French fleet concentrated in the Mediterranean to protect the vital French islands and North Africa.

By 13 July, however, affairs had quietened down. The President of France had been unimpressed with the state of affairs in the south and so had started off on his summer 'official' holiday to visit Russia with a pair of warships that would show the flag. On 23 July Admiral Sir George A. Callaghan, Commander-in-Chief of the British Home Fleet, had announced that he would disperse the fleet because the danger, if any, was over. He was planning to head for Portland for a conference of senior flag officers in which they would chew over the results of the recent mobilization. It had all been a splendid exercise, and no more than that, it seemed.

Then Austria menaced Serbia, and everything changed in a few hours.

In the Adriatic, Austria maintained three Dreadnoughts and three other battleships at Cattaro. The Germans had down there somewhere the big battle cruiser *Goeben* and the light cruiser *Breslau*.

But the situation worsened hour by hour. The Austrians

presented such sharp demands upon Serbia that to accept them would be the equivalent of surrender of sovereignty. Overnight, almost, the threat of war became very serious for the first time in years.

In London, the First Lord of the Admiralty was a youngish politician named Winston Churchill. In the months he had been in office, he had looked about him and seen that most of his senior admirals were *too* senior, and he questioned their ability to perform under the stress of battle conditions. On 24 July Winston Churchill was attending a Cabinet meeting when the Prime Minister read out the Austrian note. Since Churchill did not see how any government could accept such an ultimatum, he assumed that war must come very soon. He returned to the Admiralty in Whitehall at six o'clock that night, made up a list of points for discussion and the next day talked over the problem with the First Sea Lord. He was satisfied that England was as prepared as she would ever be. He went off for a weekend to the country. The First Sea Lord, Prince Louis of Battenberg, remained in London, reading the cables that kept arriving on his desk.

Sunday night, 26 July, affairs were so serious that Churchill reluctantly abandoned the delights of playing with his children, and hastened back to London, there to make sure the fleet was not dispersed but kept together for potential action.

The British Mediterranean Fleet was commanded by Admiral Sir Berkeley Milne. The flagship *Inflexible*, along with three other battleships, four light cruisers and fourteen destroyers, was at Alexandria. They were about to head for Malta, to meet *Indomitable* and *Duke of Edinburgh*.

Oddly enough, both Admiral E.C.T. Troubridge in *Defence* and a French cruiser were in the Adriatic, at Durazzo, taking their ceremonial part in support of a conference at Scutari where interested parties were trying to settle the vexatious Albanian question. Also at Durazzo was the *Breslau*, a small cruiser built for the German Admiralty's concept of hit-and-run cruiser warfare. She was constructed in Stettin in 1911, a 4,550-ton ship with twelve 10·5-cm guns and two torpedo tubes – the most modern of warships.

Goeben was an even greater prize – she was an armoured cruiser and the fastest vessel of her class in the Imperial German Navy. She was five times as large as the *Breslau*, displacing twenty-two thousand tons. She had a speed of twenty-eight knots, and she carried armament of ten 11-inch guns and twelve 5·9 guns, plus another dozen twenty-one pounders. As ships of their day went, these two German vessels had tremendous fuel capacity – a ship was bounded by its ability to carry fuel, as opposed to its consumption rate. *Breslau*, for example, could steam six thousand miles on fuel she carried in her bunkers, and *Goeben* was equally long-ranged for a coal burner.

As war threatened, it was apparent that these two vessels were admirably suited to become commerce raiders or to wreak havoc among older warships with their modern fighting equipment. On the scene in the Mediterranean, the senior British officers immediately saw the need to immobilize the pair, to capture or sink them at the first sign of trouble, and so stop them causing all the damage of which they were capable.

Winston Churchill, the First Lord of the Admiralty, recognized the Austrian ultimatum to Serbia as a call to war – indeed, he did not see how any mature nation could accept this 'most insolent document of its kind ever devised', and he headed for London as swiftly as he could go. Admiral Prince Louis of Battenberg was waiting for Churchill at the Admiralty, and he informed the First Lord that the political situation seemed to be deteriorating hourly. The crisis was coming about in a pyramidal fashion – weeks and days earlier no one had expected a Balkan problem to upset the peace of Europe. Now the powers were seeing life in a different light.

The Admiral had already taken steps to keep the British fleet together following its war games, instead of dispersing the ships around the British Isles, as was the usual custom. Within a few hours Churchill had the ear of the Prime Minister and then began preparing for trouble. One of the First Lord's earliest actions was to send a message to Admiral Sir Berkeley Milne, the commander in the Mediterranean, telling him to be prepared to shadow *Breslau* and *Goeben*, just in case the fears of the moment proved to have substance.

In the next three days, the British fleet began to move in battle formations, and Churchill was busy moving his ships and personnel in the manner decided best for defence. Early in August all was ready, and on 4 August Churchill sent out the telegram to begin hostilities against Germany.

Meanwhile, the German Admiralty had been planning what turned out to be the major *coup* of the first days of the war at sea. As Sir Julian Corbett put it much later, there was no decision made involving a pair of ships of any nation that had so profound an influence as this on the war that began in 1914.

The fact is also that for a long time the *Goeben* had been a thorn in the British Admiralty's side. She and *Breslau* had been sent to the Mediterranean in November 1912 to show the German flag. Because of her activity there, the British had detached the battle cruisers *Indomitable*, *Indefatigable* and *Inflexible* from home duty to look after the German vessel.

As the summer crisis came on, *Breslau* remained at Durazzo with other foreign warships, helping to prop up the shaky throne of Prince William of Wied, the ruler of Albania. Early in the summer her crew was busying itself with water polo matches against the men of *Gloucester*, a British cruiser of about her own size. *Breslau* was in good shape, ready for almost any assignment the Kaiser's Admiralty might give her. And she was trained for it – the cruisermen of Germany were ready to fight either in squadron or alone. *Breslau* was generally of the same type as the light cruiser *Emden*, which would ravage the Indian Ocean, a light vessel of four stacks and heavy armament for her size, and plenty of speed by the standards of the day.

Goeben, however, was anchored at Haifa at the other end of the Mediterranean when the news of Sarajevo came. Admiral Souchon, the commander of the German force, was attending a party at the German Consulate that day and heard the news from the Consul himself. The Germans, from the beginning, took the news much more seriously than did the British or the French, and so Admiral Souchon in a way stole a march on his potential enemies. Good that he did, for the boilers of *Goeben* that June night were in such disrepair that the engineers said that the big ship could make only seventeen knots, which was at least ten knots slower than her launching capability.

What to do? Souchon could not go home to the North Sea. His presence in the Mediterranean was more than ever necessary. Germany had no effective dockyard in East Africa, which was the closest German soil to Souchon's anchorage. The Admiral considered and put his finger on the little port of Pola in the Adriatic. The port was also the Austro-Hungarian Empire's major naval base, and Austro-Hungary and Germany were pledged in the Triple Alliance together with Italy. So the Admiral sent a message to Berlin, asking that new boiler tubes and German dockyard naval workers be sent to Pola for him. Then he went back to his ship and took the steps necessary to get the vessel in motion towards the Adriatic.

In a few days, Souchon was in Pola, and the work had begun.

Meanwhile, Souchon was also working with the Austrian naval staff to arrange a joint plan of operation in the Mediterranean. The French and British Navies could be expected to make every effort to control the Mediterranean, and without the assistance of the Italian Navy they would very likely succeed – because the German High Seas Fleet could not be detached from the North Sea, nor could it spare vessels for the south. The Austrian Navy's ships were so ancient, and its practices so outmoded, that Souchon gave very little hope of that organization's providing much assistance. Berlin approved his suggestion that the Austrian Navy move eastwards into the Aegean Sea and Turkish waters, so as to persuade the Turks to enter the war on the side of the Triple Alliance. Such a programme, if it could be successful, might also push a wavering Italy into the arms of the Germans and Austrians, and Turkey and Italy together could do much to counteract the power of Britain and France in this area.

Souchon could not afford to be caught at Pola at the northern end of the narrow Adriatic. He must get down into the Mediterranean without delay.

So much was apparent in the growing crisis at the end of July. Souchon sailed in *Goeben* and passed by Durazzo to be joined by *Breslau*, and then headed for the Sicilian port of Messina, where he coaled.

Souchon knew what he planned to do immediately on the outbreak of war. He would move towards the North African coast and destroy the French transport ships which were waiting there to carry France's Nineteenth Army Corps from Algeria to France proper. This unit would be deployed in the lines against the Germans if the ships could not be stopped. If Souchon could destroy the transport and delay shipment of the troops, the outcome might be a major blow for the fatherland at a vital moment.

Every day after 31 July it was more apparent aboard the German vessels that war was simply a matter of hours away. On 3 August Souchon's ships took on the last of their coal at Messina and sailed.

Originally, the modern Turkish army had been organized by the Germans, and Enver Pasha, one of the most prominent figures in Turkey, had been under German influence since his days in Berlin as military attaché. In the summer of 1914 he was Minister of War.

That spring and summer Baron von Wangenheim, the German Ambassador, had done everything possible to show the German friendship for the Turks – including bringing in *Goeben* for a long and impressive visit. Many were the *soirées* held aboard the ship as she lay anchored off the German Embassy at the entrance to the Golden Horn. It was part of a master plan – General Liman von Sanders and some seventy German officers were at these parties, all members of the German military mission to Turkey. One could see, as the men of *Goeben* had seen, the influence of Germany growing in the Turkish capital day after day. The Turks kept track of the whereabouts of *Goeben*, and they watched the world situation with a restless eye. The designs of the Tsars upon the Dardanelles were well known and of long standing, and the Turks were well aware of the alliance between France, Russia and Britain.

Admiral Souchon knew the general way in which the wind was blowing, although he would have been surprised in the last days of July to know precisely how specific the conversations between his own government and Enver Pasha had become.

The British did not seem to know anything. Through all the most critical days of this summer, the British Ambassador to Constantinople was absent from his post. He had chosen the strangest time to take his leave!

So it was that on 3 August, when Souchon sailed from Messina for the North African coast, a message was on the way to him regarding Turkey and the *Goeben*'s future.

For months von Sanders and others had been painting the picture of German-Turkish alliance – with Germany becoming the grand continental power of Europe, and Turkey taking over the Middle East, including northern Persia. From there, all Asia was but a few miles away, and Turkey could become to Asia what Germany was to become to Europe.

In June there was much pro-British feeling in Constantinople, and the majority of the Cabinet were definitely opposed to any war against their British friends. At this moment a guarantee of Turkish independence and a promise that Britain would restrain the Russians from attacking Turkey when the war began would probably have prevented all that came after. But Britain was supremely unconscious of the Turkish worries of the moment, and there was no one at home in Constantinople's embassy to warn the government in London of the danger that threatened.

While Admiral Souchon made ready for his operations, the German embassy in Constantinople was triply active; and as the crisis of Serbia deepened, so the Turkish Cabinet was persuaded that Britain would allow the Tsar's forces to have their way in Turkey. The fear grew day by day, until 26 July, when Austro-Hungary declared war on Serbia. Next day the Turkish Grand Vizier asked the Germans for a secret defensive and offensive alliance against Russian aggression. Berlin was quick to accept. Even as Admiral Souchon headed out from Pola, the Turkish forces were mobilizing. As he came up towards Messina, the secret treaty between Turkey and Germany was signed. As he coaled at the Sicilian port, the Turkish Navy began laying its first mines in the Dardanelles.

While Souchon headed for North Africa, at the Admiralty in Berlin an officer was framing an order to *Goeben* to rush back to Constantinople, so that Souchon could take command of the Turkish fleet and undertake to protect the Turks from their traditional Russian enemy. Admiral von Tirpitz signed the orders and sent a message to von Wangenheim in Constantinople confirming the Admiralty's intention to do anything necessary to help the Turkish government. Should the Dardanelles fall, von Tirpitz said, the World War would definitely go against the Germans.

When Admiral Souchon received his superior's order on 3 August, he should have turned immediately eastwards to run for Turkish waters, for with the presence of a large British fleet in the Mediterranean, he needed every advantage he could get in order to escape the chasing enemy. But Souchon did no such thing: he adhered to his own plan and headed for Philippeville, sending *Breslau* to bombard Bône, another Algerian port.

The attack itself was conducted on the morning of 4 August. Into Philippeville harbour came the big cruiser, both funnels belching smoke, and she sprayed the port installations with shells from her eleven-inch guns and smaller weapons. *Breslau* followed a similar pattern with her attack. As a military gesture, the attacks were unimportant – they delayed the sailing of the French convoys by fewer than four days. However, the assault served as a warning to the French and taught them to use convoys right at the outbreak of the war.

After the attack, Admiral Souchon headed back to Messina to top up with coal, ready for the dash to Constantinople. The repairs to his boilers had been less than satisfactory – this high-speed mission had made them leak again, and his coal consumption was bound to be high if he tried to run through the British fleet.

Goeben was moving along easily through the Mediterranean blue that morning, and the men of the ship were alert at war watch, for the battle cruiser had been stripped down for action at Pola, and the crew had been warned that the war had changed their whole lives.

At ten o'clock in the morning, they were about to pass above Sicily and come down on Messina. Suddenly, dead ahead, the lookouts spotted a pair of smoke plumes, and as they came up, the officers on the bridge and in the foretop identified through glasses the ships as the British battle cruisers *Indomitable* and *Indefatigable*.

The British knew that the German warship had been assaulting the French in North Africa, but it was part of the game

9

that they could not shoot until they had received Churchill's telegram. So there they were, with the enemy in their grasp, and they could do nothing at all about it.

Admiral Souchon could heave a sigh of relief – his chances against the pair of battle cruisers would have been very slim. And all they could do was shadow him. How had the British found Souchon so quickly?

When Winston Churchill had ordered the warning message to be sent from the Admiralty on 27 July, the British Mediterranean Fleet had put its operational plan into motion. That plan called for the concentration of the fleet on the big base at Malta where Admiral Sir Berkeley Milne set about removing their civilian appurtenances – such as panelling and pianos in the wardroom – and provisioning the ships for war. Their first task was to protect the French transports and make sure that the Algerian army was safe.

Learning that the German ships had coaled at Brindisi on 1 August, Rear Admiral Troubridge had taken a force of fourteen ships to the mouth of the Adriatic, but the Germans had slipped by them and reached Messina overnight. This was a sad day from the British point of view. Had they been able to bottle up the Germans in the Adriatic, then that fourteen-ship fleet of battle cruisers, armoured cruisers, light cruisers and destroyers would have been in an admirable position to end the Mediterranean war as it started. But the Germans were too canny, and there was really no chance that it could be done so easily.

Thus *Indomitable* and *Indefatigable* were sent off to watch Sicily while Admiral Troubridge and the rest of his ships remained at the mouth of the Adriatic, to keep an eye on those Austrian ships up north.

On the day that Admiral Souchon bombarded the North African coast, Admiral Milne at Malta was trying desperately to get in touch by wireless with the French, so he could co-ordinate his plans with those of Admiral Boué de Lapeyrère. All day long his operators were tapping out the call signs, waiting, tapping again – but to no avail. The atmosphere was sticky, the wireless sets were primitive and weak, and the British and French did not make contact that day.

In fact it was only because of preconceived ideas that the British found Admiral Souchon off Sicily on 4 August. Admiral Milne was certain that if war came, the Germans would head for Gibraltar and try to make a run out into the Atlantic. Perhaps their ultimate aim was to make the North Sea and return home to join the High Seas Fleet. No one seriously doubted that at some point in the coming war the matter of naval superiority would be tested in an outright encounter between the Home Fleet and the *Hochseeflotte* of the Kaiser.

British naval intelligence was convinced that the Germans were to proceed first to Majorca, where a collier was awaiting them, and then to swoop out past Gibraltar in the dead of night. So *Indomitable* and *Indefatigable* were moving at full speed for 'Gib' when they encountered the Germans just off Sicily, and had to go on, then turn around and shadow the ships of this 'potential enemy' – potential only because the hour and moment had not yet arrived.

The transition from peace to war was a hard one to make. There is no better illustration than the dilemma in which the British found themselves as they passed *Goeben*. International naval usage in peacetime indicated that Souchon should have an admiral's salute from the Royal Navy as the ships passed each other. But the British solved that problem: Admiral Souchon was not flying his command flag that day – so the British did not have to put on the charade. Souchon faced the same dilemma. His officers identified *Indomitable* as *Defence* – which was the flagship of Sir Berkeley Milne. That being the apparent case, Admiral Souchon owed the British a salute, which was a little difficult since his guns were loaded with *live* ammunition; if he fired them, he might start the war right then and there.

It was all cleared away within half an hour. *Indomitable*

was correctly identified by signal; Souchon realized that she was commanded by Captain F.W.Kennedy, not of the rank to demand a salute; and the ships passed without ado. But that was the way they were thinking in these last hours of peace; it was going to take a little while for Britons and Germans to convert to war thinking.

If there was anything Wilhelm Souchon did not want just then, it was a British shadow. He issued orders for flank speed, and slowly the German ship began to draw ahead of the British followers. The British boilers were not in any better condition than *Goeben*'s.

What was Captain Kennedy to do? He was doing everything he could to walk the narrow tightrope of duty. He was chasing the German vessel with all his skill. He was also in contact with the Admiralty in London, desperate to gain the latest information about the state of relations between Great Britain and Germany. London informed him: His Majesty's Government had issued an ultimatum to the Germans, but there had been no answer, and none was required until midnight. The Prime Minister still held a slim hope for peace, even at this eleventh hour. Kennedy was not, repeat *not*, to jeopardize that hope by any precipitate action against the *Goeben*. And so the black smoke cascaded from the funnels of *Goeben* as she sped away, and a regretful Captain Kennedy ordered his officer of the watch to cut the speed of the battle cruisers and end the upward spiral of the fuel consumption pattern. *Goeben* moved away victoriously and, well out of sight of the potential enemy, changed her course several times before heading for Messina to make the rendezvous with *Breslau* and pick up that vital extra fuel.

Midnight was a long time coming. What would Italy do? She might very well cast her lot with the German and Austrian allies, to whom she had promised so much in the Triple Alliance. But when the moment came, and Britain's war with Germany began, the Italians backed away. Rome sent a message to London, Paris, Berlin, Vienna and St Petersburg: Italy was neutral and her neutral zone extended six miles from all Italian shores.

Later, the Admiralty was to indicate that British acceptance of the six-mile limit did not include the matter of 'hot pursuit'. In hindsight it was considered that the British ships' captains and admirals ought to know better than that. But at the time, no clues were given – the Admiralty simply transmitted the Italian directive and by not commenting led the men afloat to believe that His Majesty's Government accepted the Italian interpretation of affairs.

So at midnight, Captain Kennedy moved his two ships towards Pantelleria, to rendezvous with the major force of Admiral Troubridge.

Kennedy and Troubridge might guess that Souchon was heading for Messina, but that was all the good it would do them. Troubridge sent the cruiser *Gloucester* to the southern end of the Straits of Messina to guard against a breakout, but that was the best he could do. Indeed, because Souchon arrived at Messina early, he even inveigled the Italians into getting him coal from a British collier in Messina harbour!

Had Admiral Milne sent his whole force to Messina just when suspicions were aroused, the story of *Goeben* and *Breslau* might have taken the turn that everyone expected. For Admiral Souchon did not 'smash and grab' at Messina, as everyone expected. He spent two full days coaling at that Sicilian port. On 5 and 6 August the German tars sweated and slaved between collier, lighter and the deep holds of their ships. They reduced their clothing to singlets and underpants, and some even went barefoot. The sweat poured down, for it was hot even by the standards of Sicily in August, and the wind seemed scarcely to ripple the harbour's waters. Indeed, the bottom fish came up as if to look over the proceedings, and their rising left ripples on the surface of the bay.

With their love of the dramatic, the Italians swarmed

about the German ships, calling and sometimes catcalling, warning in friendly or inimical fashion that the *tedeschi* faced the certain anger of the British fleet once the ships had moved out of Italian territorial waters.

And, of course, Souchon was a worried man. He had seen the two battle cruisers and knew that their mission must initially be to hunt him down. Outside the waters of the neutral zone, he must be prepared for any and all elements of the Mediterranean Fleet to descend upon him.

By this time Admiral Souchon had received and digested fully the instructions from Berlin that he was to proceed to Constantinople with his two ships and report to the embassy there. His problem was how to complete such a dangerous voyage. It was apparent that the British were at Malta, between him and his goal; and in order to succeed, he must run through the entire British Mediterranean Fleet, without involving himself in a battle that almost certainly would cost him both his ships.

But on 6 August the exhausted Germans decided they must leave the protected waters of Italy and chance the open sea. Each hour they delayed made it more possible that the British would bring their entire battle force up from Malta and send a line across the water that they could not escape. Time was the precious element.

Unfortunately for Souchon it was a fine moonlit night when he sailed from Messina out into the Straits, where *Gloucester* was waiting, watching and ready to report, as ordered by Admiral Troubridge. *Gloucester* could not engage or try to stop the German ships. One well placed shell from *Goeben* would blow the small cruiser out of the water. Captain Howard Kelly knew that – he was an experienced Royal Navy officer who understood his task and the sacrifices he might or might not be expected to make. At eight o'clock Souchon came under the glasses of Captain Kelly.

The German Admiral set a course to fool his enemy. Was it not logical that the two lonely ships of His Imperial

Majesty's German Navy would head for Pola, up the Adriatic? How could two ships hope to challenge the combined might of the British and French in the Mediterranean, particularly when Italy had not come to their rescue as they had been led to believe she would in time of crisis? The course was north-east; the idea was to persuade the watching British ship that Souchon was heading towards Pola and safety.

But Captain Kelly was not fooled. As the Germans passed, he waited and then pursued, watching all the time, maintaining that vital link of contact that could later help the battle forces of Admiral Milne to deal with the interlopers.

Souchon's plan was to shake the enemy by speed (how he prayed for foul weather!) and at a propitious moment to turn south-east, pass Cape Matapan and head into the Aegean Sea, bound for the entrance to the Dardanelles. He had to follow that plan – there was really no other. Each hour that Souchon spent making diversionary moves would cost him fuel. It was easy now to lament all those unanswered messages sent to Berlin about the state of his boilers in the halcyon days of peace. He had a ship in less than excellent condition, and he had to sail and perhaps fight with her as she was. Souchon was equal to the challenge. Under the eyes of *Gloucester*, he began to move. The British ship shadowed him from eight o'clock on the evening of 6 August until four-thirty on the afternoon of 7 August, through continuing fine weather. Certainly at almost any hour the German Admiral could have doubled back, with his heavy battle cruiser, and made mincemeat of *Gloucester*. But Souchon had to consider his task ahead. He had to assume that the British officer in charge of that cruiser knew his job and would make the killing of the *Gloucester* as difficult and time-consuming as possible – even if Souchon could catch her. He had to consider fuel, speed and the disposition of the British fleet. Souchon opted against the destruction of his shadow. At one point he yielded enough to send *Breslau* to destroy

Gloucester but Captain Kelly fled, using speed and manœuvrability, keeping just on the horizon. He did, of course, lose *Goeben*, much to the satisfaction of Admiral Souchon. Yet when *Breslau* was called back, Captain Kelly managed to follow her and after all the waste of coal, there was the little fleet, *Goeben* steaming angrily, *Breslau* in her wake, and off on the edge of the horizon, the shadow of *Gloucester*, still watching and following.

All this while, for nearly twenty hours, Captain Kelly had been sending regular messages to Admiral Milne and Admiral Troubridge to inform them of the progress of the Germans. He would drop back, come up, observe, drop back and come up again, estimating courses and speeds, and no changes the Germans made seemed to stop his observations.

Admiral Milne must decide what course of action he was to take with the main fleet. His orders were to protect the French from attack – and who knew what other German ships might be heading into the Mediterranean, what U-Boats might be about, or what the Austrian Navy could be up to? Milne took a very narrow view of his orders. So he steamed at eight knots from Malta towards Sicily, making sure that he was keeping on a line that separated the German vessels from any attempt at attack on the French ships that were preparing to move the Algerian armies to France and thus into action on the Western front.

Admiral Troubridge, the second in command of the fleet, had come out in *Defence*, and he now had with him four armoured cruisers and eight destroyers. His thinking was a great tribute to the Imperial German Navy – Troubridge did not believe he had sufficient force at hand to challenge the *Goeben* with her escort *Breslau*. There is the difference between a Milne and a Troubridge on the one hand, and a Nelson or a Beatty on the other! As the Royal Navy's overseers were learning and were to learn, the qualities that made a fine peacetime naval officer were not necessarily those that made a successful fighting commander.

Hour after hour Captain Kelly shadowed and waited to hear from his superiors that they were closing in to do battle. But instead, Milne and Troubridge decided to give up the chase and called *Gloucester* back from the mission. There, in sight of the enemy, the British naval command had foundered on its own conservatism. Admiral Souchon sailed on, not knowing for hours that he had been given grace by the timidity of his new-found enemies.

Had Milne and Troubridge regretted their decision and reconsidered it, they could still have attacked. For when Admiral Souchon had run the gauntlet and was approaching the Dardanelles, Berlin did to him what shore commands often did to their fighting men: he received orders to stop, to approach the island of Denusa, east of Naxos, and there to wait – exposed – for the appearance of a collier that would give him fuel and lead him into the safety of the Dardanelles.

Souchon's intent was to rush the Dardanelles, to speed through the minefield whose location he said he knew and to move through the Bosphorus into the Black Sea, where he would ravage the Russian ships that he knew to be inferior to his own great cruiser. But he was delayed, for Souchon was a good servant of His Majesty and would not disobey a direct order.

However, Admiral Milne failed to take the chance. Some-one at the Admiralty slipped up and sent a message to the effect that Britain was at war with Austria (which was not true at the moment: it did not come until 13 August), and Milne sent all his ships to cover the exit from the Adriatic, once again to protect those French ports and French supply-lines. So while the Mediterranean fleet should have been scurrying eastwards to repair the mistake of the beginning, it was sitting off the Adriatic coast, doing little.

The time gained let the Germans in the east do more or less as they wished. The Turks were nervous – they had not antici-pated war with Britain when they set all these wheels in motion to secure German guarantees of Turkish freedom.

Now the Germans in Constantinople were aggressive and open in their pressures on the Turks. When the *Goeben* and *Breslau* arrived at the Sedd-el-Bahr, at the entrance to the Dardanelles, they asked permission to enter Turkish waters, as they had been instructed by Berlin to do. The Germans were actually in control of the Turkish defence forces by that time – General von Sanders had done his work well – and so Germans gave Germans permission to enter Turkish waters. The peace party in Constantinople, which had been wavering, was overcome. The Turkish government also issued an order denying the Allies the right to enter the Dardanelles, as the Germans had done. So *Goeben* and *Breslau* were safe from pursuit.

Poor Admiral Milne – he had been tried at the outbreak of war and found wanting. Winston Churchill had no sympathy for a man of inaction. Had Milne swept into action and sunk the *Goeben* and the *Breslau*, Churchill would undoubtedly have stood up for him no matter what the consequences. But in Milne's failure, he lost sail. He was never again employed in command during the war.

As for Admiral Troubridge, he was so near and yet so far from battle in his thinking. He was actually courtmartialled for negligence of duty in failing to pursue and engage the German ships. He was acquitted of wrongdoing and later put in charge of a contingent of naval guns – but what a sad end for a sea commander. He was never again given command of a fighting force of ships.

Indeed, in view of the international repercussions of the escape of *Goeben* and *Breslau* in these opening hours of the war, it was remarkable that the two commanders were dealt with as lightly as they were. For the whole world had the news within a week – and the Germans had a major propaganda victory. Even more important and more dreadful from the British point of view was the repercussion on the diplomatic scene. The Turks were tremendously impressed by the feat of the Germans, and in a matter of days Turkey was seen to be virtually in the German camp. Now the eyes of Churchill and other war leaders were cast towards the Dardanelles in a manner that the British would not have considered had mighty *Goeben* not sought her refuge there.

2   The War

From the dawn of military history in the Middle East and Europe, the world has been aware of the vital importance of the Dardanelles.

'Who is to have Constantinople?' was the question asked by Napoleon when he set about his conquest of the western world. And the question was as valid in Winston Churchill's mind in the autumn and winter of 1914 as it had ever been in Napoleon's, for in the city and the Dardanelles, Churchill and other leaders saw the chance to end the war of the Germans and Austrians very quickly by entering the 'back door'.

The door at the moment was closed. The arrival of *Goeben* and *Breslau* at Constantinople, when all the world said it would never happen, had thrust the Turks into the arms of the Germans.

The Turks were already wavering. In the summer, the British had come to a decision at home that was totally understandable to an outside world but not much liked in Constantinople. The Turks had previously ordered two new battleships from British shipyards, ships that were built largely by public subscription in Turkey. One of the ships was ready for delivery in July 1914, when the Serbian crisis was heating up, and the Turkish crew had actually reached England to take over the vessel. Only then was Turkey told that the two vessels would not be delivered but would be taken over by the Royal Navy.

By the time the *Goeben* and *Breslau* arrived in Constantinople, the German propaganda and military machines of

Turkey were in full operation. Ambassador von Wangenheim purchased the newspaper *Ikdam* and made of it a German organ. The Germans bought editors and editorial space in other newspapers. The Turkish government ordered censorship and the slanting of the news so as to become pro-German. Kaiser Wilhelm suddenly became the most prominent foreigner in all Turkey.

On 10 August, the British set up the usual cry that Turkey's obligation as a neutral power meant that she must force the two German vessels to intern or leave the Straits at once. The Turks replied suavely that they had bought the two vessels from Germany to replace the two held in captivity by the British. The British then suggested that the crews of the German ships be sent back to Germany. Oh yes, said the Turks, and Admiral Souchon and his men doffed their Imperial war caps and donned fezes. They never went anywhere – they were now part of the Turkish Navy.

The British interest in all this activity was hampered considerably by Turkish action. On 15 August the British naval mission under Vice-Admiral A.H.Limpus was suddenly deprived of its independent status and told that if it continued to remain in Turkey at all, it would have to operate under the Ministry of Marine. A week later Admiral Souchon was appointed Commander-in-Chief of the Turkish Navy.

Did this mean that the Turks were allying themselves with Germany against the west? asked the British Ambassador at the Sublime Porte.

Not at all, said the Turks. Turkey was neutral.

How neutral – a lesson for future generations of politicians who could see nations leaning one way and talking another. For the Turks now sowed new lanes of mines in the Dardanelles and set up new Hotchkiss guns to cover the waters. The Dardanelles had been made 'impregnable'. German marines and German soldiers were moving into the fortifications along the Turkish coast, particularly along the seaward side.

British and French ships were detained at Constantinople and searched, and their wireless sets were destroyed so that they could not send messages about German activity. Altogether it was an odd sort of neutrality and not one that fooled the British very much. But it was to Britain's advantage to maintain the charade as long as possible. It was possible that a declaration of war by Turkey might be followed by an attack on Suez by some of the Turkish naval forces, reinforced and led by the Germans who were actually in control of both army and navy.

The British were pliable but tough. They announced that if Turkey would revert to real neutrality, they would guarantee the country's safety from any Russian attack. They also announced that until the German crews left those two warships, *Goeben* and *Breslau*, the British would not recognize the 'sale' to Turkey and furthermore that no Turkish warships were to move out into the Mediterranean until this change was effected. A British squadron sat off the entrance to the Straits and watched, to be sure no Germans came out in Turks' clothing.

By 1 September affairs were moving fast. Admiral Limpus announced that his naval mission was becoming a laughing-stock, because the Germans were everywhere in authority. So Churchill ordered the removal of the mission from Turkish soil but gave Limpus both honour and a huge task, by appointing him to control the British Dardanelles Squadron.

What a strange, old-fashioned war it was in the beginning. Could anyone imagine that a naval officer, given a plum command in which he could use to the fullest the information he had been given by an ungrateful power, would refuse the command? Limpus did, on the grounds that it would be ignoble to use the 'inside information' he had secured in Turkey against the Turks. And Whitehall sympathized. The cost of this decision – the loss of Limpus's special insights into Turkish defences and the Turkish mentality – was to be very high. Before the affair was ended, it would cost thousands of Allied lives.

The German interest in having Turkey enter the war was overwhelming. The Russians at this point in history were doing a large trade with England and other western European countries through the Black Sea and the Dardanelles. Southern Russian produced oil for British industry (and the war machine), and food products from Russia had become staples in the western European diet. Britain would be hard put to replace the trade lost if the Dardanelles were closed.

There was another reason. It was Germany's intent to lock Russia off from her allies. By closing the Dardanelles on the south and the Baltic Sea on the north, she could do just that. The contact would be lost, and Russia's ability to secure war *matériel* from the heavily industrialized nations would be wiped out. Thus the German effort in Constantinople was worth every *pfennig* it cost and every danger it posed.

As affairs continued to deteriorate Winston Churchill observed, with the peculiar combination of cynicism and optimism that marked his political character, that British diplomacy was bound to fail in Constantinople. He had already begun looking for a way to re-open the Dardanelles. His first idea was to employ a Greek army, trading on the traditional enmity of Greek for Turk. But by September he had still reached no decision.

The Germans certainly controlled the Turkish defences. General von Sanders had been the single most important figure in Turkish War Ministry circles since December 1913, when he became a Marshal and Inspector General of the Turkish Army. He came to find a Turkish Army that was almost totally unprepared for war, but, using the Prussian methods, in a matter of six months he had begun to turn things about.

As for the Turkish Navy, before the coming of *Goeben* and

Breslau, it had consisted of three old battleships, two lightly armoured cruisers, two torpedo cruisers, eight destroyers, ten torpedo boats and seven minelayers. *Goeben* and *Breslau* were years ahead of these vessels in terms of modernity and effectiveness. Indeed, so great was the disparity that in September, when the two German ships were made the backbone of the Turkish fleet, Admiral Souchon relegated *all* Turkish ships to the reserve – and only later realized that he could not function without some of them, ancient as they might be. *Goeben*'s name was changed to *Yavuz Sultan Selim* (*Sultan Selim the Dread*) and *Breslau* was called *Midilli*, after the island of Mytilene in the Aegean.

During September and October, Admiral Souchon worked on the organization and training of his navy. He brought the best Turkish ship forward; she was the *Messudiyeh*, an elderly battleship. He added one lightly armoured or protected cruiser to the force, two of the torpedo cruisers and the eight destroyers. He had a very definite plan in mind.

During this time, the British had not been idle either. A British squadron operated just offshore, watching and waiting. The escape of the *Goeben* and *Breslau*, with all its attendant publicity, had created such a scandal in Britain that most attention was paid to these vessels. The First British Cruiser Squadron was on guard, and this meant among other ships the *Indomitable*, whose Captain Kennedy had encountered *Goeben* off Sicily on the very day that war with Germany broke out and yet had been reduced to impotence by the train of events that day.

Kennedy had not forgotten this. If there was any one thing that dominated his mind, it was the presence of the *Goeben* in Turkish waters. Kennedy and his brother officers stood guard outside the straits and waited, trying to think of a way in which they could flush the German enemy who had made a monkey of them a few days before.

On 16 August, Captain Kennedy put pen to paper to suggest to his commander of the First Cruiser Squadron an audacious plan for dealing with the *Goeben* and *Breslau*. He wanted to dispatch a British naval officer in plain clothes to the settlement of Chanak. A merchant ship they had stopped was heading there; it was an ideal opportunity for the Navy to spy out the proceedings of the Germans and the Turks at the Dardanelles. If the higher echelon approved, would the commander please telegraph as follows: 'Flour cannot be bought here.'

That message in hand, Captain Kennedy would put his men aboard the merchantman and send the vessel on its way. In a matter of days or hours, this trusted officer would return with the story of *Goeben* and *Breslau* and tell the squadron what it had to face.

Britain and Turkey were still at uneasy peace, as this plan unfolded. Unfortunately higher echelon did not think much of it. Kennedy sat and fumed some more. Who could ever forget the sight of *Goeben* on the eve of war above Sicily, steaming along so arrogantly and so certain that she could not be touched by the two ships that might have dealt with her in a hurry?

On 16 August, Captain Kennedy was cheered to learn that Vice-Consul C.E. Palmer had reported on the Dardanelles. He did not much like what he heard: *Goeben* and *Breslau* were taking on coal, said the Consul. Did that mean they were coming out to fight? Not at all – they had both been re-named, said the Consul, and were now Turkish ships.

Palmer was worried. He was now being watched by German agents and, more important, by the officials of the Sublime Porte, who suspected that the Consul was doing his diplomatic duty and reporting to the British forces offshore. It would be most difficult for Palmer to continue to send messages. He had no codes. How could he continue to report on the German vessels without arousing the suspicion and enmity of the Turks, who were now claiming the ships as their own and would resent any implications to the contrary?

Captain Kennedy was a most resourceful man. He devised a

lengthy code of the unbreakable variety – because the words and phrases were not transpositions but depended entirely on the knowledge of the code:

> Are you better? = *Goeben* ready for sea
> Wife better = *Breslau* ready for sea
> Many thanks = War with Turkey
> Mother improving = German ships sailed

And so the messages began to come again, in varied and strange ways. Never was there a more unusual and fancied correspondence between two men than between the Consul and Captain Kennedy. The British are a reticent people, and strangers seldom inquire much about the relatives of other strangers – but Kennedy was forever wondering how Mother was faring and how Consul Palmer's wife was getting on. Such solicitude!

The Consul was not the only person concerned. In Constantinople Ambassador Sir Louis Mallet was keeping London informed of all he managed to glean about the German vessels and the constant arrival of German soldiers, sailors and specialists for the big guns that guarded the approaches to the Dardanelles and that narrow passage, too. Sir Louis opened the speculation – would it be possible to force the Dardanelles, get into the Black Sea and maintain control so that the Germans and their apparent new allies could not shut the door again?

The commander of the unit, Vice-Admiral S.H. Carden, laid out Winston Churchill's anxieties and the feeling of the Admiralty in Whitehall one September day, when it was certain that the Germans had indeed transferred *Goeben* and *Breslau* to the Turkish flag. The Admiral informed the squadron: 'Your sole duty is to sink the *Goeben* and the *Breslau*.'

But how? They had to get at the ships before they could sink them, and they could not get at them as long as Britain and Turkey continued in a normal peaceful state of official relations, no matter how un-neutrally the Turks were behaving in Constantinople and in the build-up of the military forces, navy and forts under German leadership.

Inside the Turkish perimeter, Consul Palmer continued his studies, and, as instructed by his naval friends, he concentrated very heavily on discovering the secrets of the Dardanelles.

That passage, from its mouth at Cape Helles to the Sea of Marmara, is forty-one miles long; on the west it is dominated along the whole by the heights of the Gallipoli peninsula; on the eastern, or Asiatic shore, the heights are much less spectacular.

As all the British military knew, at the beginning of the European war only the mouth of the Straits was fortified: a handful of installations ran the four-mile course from the north of Kephez Bay to the narrows at Chanak, from where Captain Kennedy had wanted to send his naval spy.

At the mouth, the Straits of the Dardanelles are four thousand yards wide, or a little more than two miles. They broaden out as they go, until they reach a width of four and a half miles about five miles upstream, at Eren Keui Bay. The water then begins to narrow, till it reaches Kephez Point, eleven miles from the entrance, where it is 1·7 miles wide. The Straits open up again until they get to the narrows of Chanak, and here, fourteen miles from the entrance, the width is only sixteen hundred yards. That is the critical point for ships passing, for after this point the water opens up again, until it reaches the Sea of Marmara and Gallipoli some twenty-three miles away.

In August the outer defences of this system consisted of two forts near the edge of the Gallipoli peninsula and two others on the Asiatic shore. They had only nineteen guns among them, and of these, as Consul Palmer learned, only four were really worth talking about, because of various reasons dealing with the decay and corruption of the Turkish forces, the other guns could not be made to fire. And the four guns that could operate had a range of only sixteen thousand yards.

If one could force the forts, which seemed entirely possible just then to Palmer and other observers, then the road upstream for the first ten miles was totally undefended. One had to reach Kephez Point to find four works, with a fifth on the opposite European shore. And these were small guns, whose major task was to protect the minefield from interference by small craft. On 3 August, Palmer had noted, the Turks laid a field of mines – a single line between Kephez Point and the other shore. There were no mines at the mouth of the Strait, so the British vessels could get in safely enough and then take action.

The third and final defence force in the Dardanelles was the Inner Defence line at the Narrows. Here the Turks had collected a large number of guns, including howitzers and field guns. On the European shore stood five forts; on the Asiatic shore stood six, and the total was seventy-two guns. Five fourteen-inch guns and three 9·4-inch guns could fire up to seventeen thousand yards but the remainder of the guns could not reach beyond ten thousand yards. To sum up: of all the guns at the Dardanelles at the opening of the war, only fourteen were modern long-range weapons.

But that was in August – before the Germans took a hand.

From Berlin in September came Vice-Admiral von Usedom with some five hundred men who would be assigned to the Dardanelles and Bosphorus forts. Admiral Merten and a detachment of German marines went to Chanak to take over the Narrows forts. And while in August the German inspectors of General von Sanders had reported the forts all along the waterway in terrible condition, by mid-September von Usedom could report to Constantinople that the Narrows forts were ready to fight, and that progress was being made to modernize and prepare the others.

Von Usedom was a busy man. In October, while Admiral

Souchon prepared the better ships of the fleet, von Usedom stripped down the armament of some of the older vessels and brought the guns ashore to strengthen the forts. There was no time to worry about bringing new weapons from the German and Austrian supplies, even if the transport could be arranged. Working with what he had, von Usedom prepared. Somewhere he found another 145 mines, and these were laid in the waters around the coast. Searchlights and small guns were put on the shore to protect against enemy sweepers that might try to destroy the minefields. Towards the end of October, Admiral von Usedom could give the High Command some encouraging news.

Just at that time Admiral Souchon set out on a remarkable adventure. He upped anchor with his force of German ships and old Turkish vessels and, without telling a soul except Enver Pasha, the most pro-German of all the ministers of the throne, he set sail for the Black Sea. On he went, past von Usedom's forts, the Turkish flag flying bravely above the vessels, the officers of the *Goeben* and *Breslau* wearing their fezes.

They steamed to Sevastopol and opened fire on the Russian port, still flying the Turkish flags. There had been no declaration of war, no indication that the Turks were ready to start hostilities, but the German Admiral forced the issue, destroying Russian ships and shipping facilities, and leaving a pall of smoke above Sevastopol as they moved to Novorossiysk. Still no declaration of war – still another bombardment of flame and steel to wreck ships and cost lives and property. And then Admiral Souchon turned back towards Turkey, the die cast. By 1 November 1914, Russia was at war with Turkey, goaded by the unprovoked attack of the German-led naval force. And Britain was almost immediately at war with Turkey too, honouring her alliance.

There was a problem of defence, Admiral von Usedom had to admit, as the hostilities began. The forts along the Dardanelles might be in better condition than before, but they were woefully short of ammunition: they had only enough shells for the big guns to withstand one major attack.

The British Ambassador burned his secret papers, picked up his passports at the Foreign Office and left Constantinople. The time for talk had ended. The time for action had begun.

On 2 November, the Admiralty ordered the Cruiser Squadron to bombard the Turkish forts. On the night of 2 November Admiral Carden issued his orders to the big ships, and next morning *Indefatigable* and *Indomitable* complied. The latter, for example, was a six-year-old ship that had been assigned to the Dardanelles blockade force early on. She was 567 feet long and displaced seventeen thousand tons. She carried eight twelve-inch guns, two dozen smaller weapons and thirty torpedoes that could be launched through five tubes. She was belt-armoured (some of it ten inches thick), and her decks were protected by armour as much as two-and-a-half inches thick. Her Babcock boilers were driven by Parsons turbines that generated forty-one thousand horsepower, which meant twenty-five knots on her four screws at flank speed. She was one of the first of the new battle cruisers and a fearsome instrument of destruction for her time.

There was no particular point in the bombardment of the Dardanelles forts, except to punish the Turks and point out to them what a dreadful mistake they had made in their choice of allies. The ships stood off at long range, well out of reach of the Turkish (German-manned) guns, and, like tennis players, they lobbed high explosive shells into the defences and the guns of the forts at the entrance to the Dardanelles. The action began just after dawn, at 5.45 in the morning. *Indefatigable* and *Indomitable* pasted Fort Sedd-el-Bahr, and very early on they found the fort's magazine. There was a flash and a tremendous roar, quite audible aboard the ships miles away, and then a cloud of grey smoke began to plume towards the sky, while debris, which looked like tiny stones and sticks, shot up to five hundred feet as in a geyser and then rained down upon the fort and its environs.

The French warships *Suffren* and *Vérité* also moved into action that morning, choosing the forts at Kum Kale and Yeni Shehr. They set fires as well, and when it was over, they accounted a good day's work. For they had accomplished their mission, these ships of the Allied joint navy that would undertake the battle of the Dardanelles. They had tested the forts and found them anything but impregnable. The lesson was read very carefully back in London.

3 Call to Battle

From the point of view of the Germans in Constantinople, the Allies could not have handed them a better present than the long-range bombardment of the forts at the entrance to the Dardanelles. General von Sanders and Admiral Souchon could watch with grave equanimity as it occurred.

The firing had lasted only twenty minutes. When it was finished, Javad Pasha, the commander of the forts, received the reports: he learned of carnage. The forts at Sedd-el-Bahr were totally destroyed in those lucky shots that had struck the magazines. The explosion of the main magazine had smashed all the guns – some of them were blown up and every one of them was out of action for days or weeks. What Admiral von Usedom had been saying was now recognized as truth: the Outer Defences were the most vulnerable of all the protection of the Dardanelles. Given the new big guns and the new British ships that mounted them, the enemy could stand offshore, out of range, and destroy the forts as quickly as they might be rebuilt.

Before this moment, consideration had been given to mounting more and better guns at the Outer Defences, but this plan was seen in Constantinople as self-defeating, and the defenders decided to concentrate their efforts on the Inner Defences. They would concentrate in particular on the minefield.

As the guns arrived overland from Germany, they were distributed on each side of the Strait, between Dardanos Fort and the entrance. Large grey howitzers, drawn by horses, were moved into place. Barges took them across the narrow water to the European side. On both sides the Germans supervised the building of revetments and concealing earthworks that fitted in against the craggy sides of the hills. The guns were as well concealed as German military expertise could make them. The object was to deny the British and French an anchorage inside the mouth of the passage. The howitzers were not going to sink any enemy warships perhaps, but they would harry the invaders, prevent them from destroying the inner forts at long range and disturb their attempts to run through the minefields, or to sweep the mines.

Admiral von Usedom also undertook a campaign of guile. He ordered a number of old weapons to be brought to this area, small guns for the most part, which were equipped with the smokiest black powder that could be found in all of Islam. These guns were not expected to destroy any ships or even create any casualties – their purpose was to draw the fire of the enemy and capture his attention so the other guns could do their work.

As the days and weeks followed, the Allied fleet outside the Dardanelles sat fretfully quiet, for there were no further orders to action from London. On the outbreak of war, Consul Palmer came aboard the *Indefatigable* to visit his friend Captain Kennedy. The Captain reported to his Admiral that Palmer was full of valuable information about the Turks and their war effort, and the whole Dardanelles disposition. But the ships stayed well outside range and did not even come back up to that point, about ten miles offshore, from which the eight vessels of the first bombardment had worked.

In London Winston Churchill had become an outright advocate of strong action against the Turks. By moving around and forcing the war against the 'underbelly', the Allies would relieve pressure on the Russians, who needed so many devices of modern warfare that they could not produce themselves, and divert much of the German and Austrian effort by forcing them to fight on three fronts.

33

Already in this post-harvest season, the Allies in the west were also suffering from the cut-off of trade through the Black Sea and Mediterranean. Russian wheat was held up in Russia and did not reach London. Vladivostok and Archangel, the two northern ports, were glutted with trade goods. The narrow artery of the Trans-Siberian railroad could not serve the Black Sea ports, nor was it sensible to move goods from southern Russia up north, against the tide, as it were.

In London that autumn, the effects were felt in the City. Russia could not pay for the goods she needed, and so the *rouble* fell. Russian bonds and Russian stocks began to depreciate. A Russian oil company declared a 'profit' but could not sell its oil, and then could not pay its foreign stock holders because of the shortage of money. In the year before the war, one third of all Russian exports, valued at more than 550 million *roubles*, had moved by ship through the Dardanelles. The Black Sea region was the granary of Europe in the days of the Tsars.

The Greeks, it seemed, might come into the war, a prospect which excited Winston Churchill so much that he began working to this end. But the Foreign Office did not like the idea, and at that moment there were no other troops available for the Middle East.

Churchill held that Turkey must be kept in check by an attack on the Gallipoli peninsula. Otherwise the Turks were certain to be goaded by the Germans into an attack on Egypt. The generals held that a Gallipoli operation would require at least sixty thousand men, and there were not that many uncommitted to the Western Front. But in November Australian troops began to arrive in Egypt, and here, thought Churchill, was a beginning – two divisions that might be used to strike Gallipoli.

Churchill wanted it done immediately. Lord Kitchener took a more conservative view and considered all the difficulties of moving an army and inaugurating a whole new front for the war. The First Lord of the Admiralty wanted action, a 'master stroke', but if this was genius, it was not shared entirely in Whitehall, and so in November the plan was put aside.

No naval effort could yet be launched against the Dardanelles. The First Cruiser Squadron was all the Admiralty could spare in October and November, for uncommitted ships of the British Royal Navy at that time simply did not exist. First, there was the Home Fleet, which kept a bulldog eye on the Germans across the Channel and guarded the North Sea approaches against submarines and raiders. Second, a good portion of the naval force was tied up in the Far East and the Indian Ocean, where the light cruiser *Emden* was ravaging the waters around India, and the light cruiser *Königsberg* was doing a similar harrying job off the Rufiji and Zanzibar.

But even worse than that was the development at the beginning of November in the far-away waters of the Pacific. Two squadrons of British cruisers around the Americas were searching for Admiral Graf von Spee and the German East Asia Cruiser Squadron. Indeed, in September the Dardanelles force had actually been decreased in order to send more ships after von Spee and his dangerous squadron of armoured and light cruisers. The heavy cruiser *Defence* was detached from the Dardanelles operation and directed to South America to reinforce Rear-Admiral Sir Christopher Cradock and the cruiser squadron searching the Pacific and Southern waters for the Germans. *Defence* never arrived on station because of a new panic – von Spee was seen off Apia, and in the confusion that followed, the Admiralty set up a whole new system of traps that diverted *Defence* at a vital moment. Like *Goeben* and *Breslau*, Admiral von Spee's *Scharnhorst* and *Gneisenau*, aided by the light cruisers *Dresden*, *Leipzig* and *Nürnberg*, were causing the British and French tremendous trouble. The shadows of *Goeben* and *Breslau* were still hovering over the entire British fleet, for Admiral Cradock had observed what happened to Admirals Milne and Troubridge after the two German ships slipped through the cordon and escaped into Turkish waters. Cradock wrote Troubridge a letter of sympathy for the rough manner in which he had been treated by the Admiralty. If and when Cradock found von Spee, he told his friend, it was clear that the squadron would be expected to engage and fight to the end against the Germans, no matter what the disparity in forces.

In September, Cradock was off the west coast of South America, waiting for *Defence*. He was aboard the flagship *Good Hope*, a heavy cruiser, and he had the heavy cruiser *Monmouth* with him, plus the light cruiser *Glasgow* and the auxiliary cruiser *Otranto*. It was not enough, as everyone realized, and so the old battleship *Canopus* was also assigned to Cradock and sent on its lumbering way. Old *Canopus* had been commissioned in 1899, and she had served all over the world from China to the Atlantic, most recently as guardship at St Vincent, a task for which she was well suited. She was moving around to join Cradock, but only at seventeen knots which compared unfavourably, as everyone knew, to the twenty-three knots of von Spee's slowest ship. In mid-September the movement of *Defence* was stopped when the Admiralty heard of *Emden*'s superbly destructive activity in the Indian Ocean. But *Canopus* was sent on.

Thus it was that every single naval action, and even rumours and reports, had an effect on every other action that emanated from Whitehall these nervous days. No order was sacrosanct – it might be changed the next day.

But what Cradock knew, what had come from the incident of *Goeben* and *Breslau*, was that Churchill and the Government demanded not duty, but gallantry. If Cradock came upon von Spee – no matter what the circumstances – he was expected to be Nelsonian and fight. The lesson of *Goeben* was there for all to see in Milne's disgrace.

On 14 October *Canopus* had been despatched, and so Whitehall ordered Cradock to go to the west coast with his squadron and gave him the bad news that *Defence* would be joining his opposite number, Admiral Stoddart, who was to scour the east coast of South America for the Germans. Churchill and the others in London knew that they were giving Cradock an impossible job – but impossible jobs were the role of the Navy in these opening days of the war, when the thin line was stretched across the world. Cradock was well aware of what was expected of him.

But *Canopus* very nearly collapsed on the Admiral. She was in desperate condition, her boilers all wheezing and leaking, and instead of her seventeen knots, she was making about twelve, which completely exasperated Admiral Cradock. Whitehall heard and was sublimely indifferent to the Admiral's problem.

When Cradock set out around the Horn, he left *Canopus* to make her way through the Strait of Magellan. He asked for *Defence*, but the Sea Lords denied him the ship. So Cradock set out to meet his destiny with a squadron far under strength, and he also knew, as did his officers, that the end was near. Two of the lieutenant commanders of *Monmouth* sent off farewell letters to their wives. On 1 November Cradock found von Spee's squadron and, obeying orders, attacked. *Canopus* never arrived in time, and the odds were tremendous. By nightfall, nine hundred officers and men, and the Admiral, had gone down aboard the sinking *Good Hope*, joined by those two lieutenant commanders and five hundred other officers and men of *Monmouth*. *Glasgow* and *Otranto* got away, and *Canopus* was saved, to be turned back shortly towards the Middle East to join the blockading forces at the Dardanelles.

Thus were intertwined the fates of all the ships at sea. But in November and December, while *Canopus* was yet lurking in South American waters, of as little use to Admiral Stoddart as she had been to Admiral Cradock, Winston Churchill still could not launch any meaningful naval assault on the Dardanelles. Not until Stoddart had vanquished von Spee could any ships be spared from the South American search. So

37

Vice-Admiral Carden was still alone at the Dardanelles with his little squadron, reinforced by some submarines and small ships but not yet given aircraft needed for observation or the force that he must have to undertake anything important against Turkey and the *Goeben* and the *Breslau*. 'Wait' was the watchword.

4 The Glorious Episode

Admiral Carden was nearly as anxious as Captain Kennedy and the other officers of the squadron that besieged Constantinople from the Aegean Sea.

The Staff and Lieutenant Commander G.H.Pownall were studying the idea of an attack on the *Goeben* and the *Breslau*. Would it not be possible for a submarine to enter the Dardanelles, avoid the shore batteries by submerging, avoid the minefields and find one of the capital ships and sink it? Lieutenant Commander Pownall was certain that it was possible. If gallantry was wanted, then let them give the submarines a chance – and of course he wanted to do the job himself.

But with the greatest of restraint, Pownall gave up the chance of personal glory. He was submarine commander and under him served all these bright-eyed young lieutenants who were also eagerly awaiting the moment when they might find glory by serving king and country. So Pownall backed away, to his undying credit as a commander and his personal despair of the moment. After much discussion and consideration, he chose Lieutenant Norman D. Holbrook and the *B-11* for the task.

Since 1910, the Mediterranean flotilla had been accompanied by submarines, although there was an almost continual argument about the manner in which these craft should be employed. Some senior officers did not want them around at all, others considered the submarine useful only for limited scouting activity for the fleet; and still others, particularly those who manned the submersible craft,

39

considered them potentially the most effective part of the 'whole bloomin' Navy'.

To Malta in 1910 came the submarines *B-9*, *B-10* and *B-11*. Already, even four years before the war, they were outmoded devices, not at all to be compared with the sleek new *U*-boats of the Germans or the *E* class of the Royal Navy, which displaced eight hundred tons, as compared to the 313 tons of the *B* class. Nor did the little boats have the latest amenities. They were 135 feet long, 13·5 feet in beam; they had a theoretical surface speed of thirteen knots and a theoretical submerged speed of nine knots, and any captain who coaxed that out of them was already a heroic figure. So were the men who served in these cranky, evil smelling and often airless craft.

Lieutenant Holbrook had been in command of *B-11* since the end of 1913. He was familiar with the little submarine and understood her treacherous petrol-burning engine (the danger of explosion was never far away) and her two eighteen-inch torpedo tubes.

When the cruiser squadron came out from Malta and set up its base at Mudros on the island of Lemnos, the submarines came tagging along behind, followed by the old depot ship *Hindu Kush*. This ship was the headquarters of Lieutenant Commander Pownall and also the tender for the submarine flotilla. It was not long before the French sent out three submarines, and the word came from Whitehall that they would soon be joined by the Gibraltar contingent, *B-6* and *B-7*. All the more reason that some action ought to be launched before the place crowded up with volunteers, for Lieutenant Commander Brodie, of the Gibraltar station would be as eager for his boys as Pownall was for his own.

Lieutenants Warburton and Gravener, the commanders of the other two *B*-boats off Mudros, argued endlessly that they ought to have a chance and were assured that they would have their opportunities in time. The submarine officers, then, began to plan the operation they would carry out.

The first thing needed by any submarine venturing into the mined waters of the Dardanelles was some kind of bow-cap to turn away the mines, so the submarine would not be blown sky high on its approach through the channel. The officers sketched out what they thought would be appropriate, and on 3 December *B-11* came up alongside *Blenheim*, for the construction of the guard that would prevent the mine moorings from fouling the submarine's hydroplanes. These flanges would push the mine cables clear. Holbrook was then ready for the job. He had new batteries in his submarine (that was one reason why *B-11* was chosen for the task). He was as familiar with the territory as any Briton on hand – for in pursuit he had moved twice into the Turkish waters, stalking Turkish gunboats.

Sitting down in the wardroom of *Hindu Kush*, the submariners clustered around charts and compared notes and knowledge. Even though the decision had been made to send *B-11*, there was a constant press for more activity on the part of the other submariners, particularly the French, who were very sensitive to service under an English command here at the Dardanelles. So the promise was made: the French would have the very next chance. The wounded feelings assuaged; calm was restored to the wardroom. The major obstacle to submarine success was the minefield, which by this time consisted of five lines of moored mines. But the mines were finite objects – and there was a much greater danger to the *B*-class submarines with their small size and relative instability.

Then came the discussion of the new problem that all the submariners had observed in these waters. The currents seemed to be designed to assist the Turkish defenders, for at ten fathoms the undersea men had discerned a stratum of fresh water which was much denser than the salt water of the area and which made it difficult for a submarine to maintain its depth and manœuvre successfully. Not only was the fresh water stream inimical in its density, but it was a powerful current running into the sea, and it could prove expensive in terms of the precious battery power that must be used underwater. The intelligent idea was to stay above the fresh flow, or get under it, but in any event to get away from it as quickly as humanly possible.

On 12 December everything was in order. Higher authority had agreed that the submariners' idea was well within the assignment Winston Churchill had given Admiral Carden: to destroy those German battleships no matter how it was done. And Carden knew that any success would be much appreciated at home. So the permissions were given, and the little submarine was as ready as she would ever be for the task, as were Lieutenant Holbrook and his men. For several days he had practised diving and trimming the craft, until he was satisfied that he was doing as well as he possibly could. He was going to be diving in a tideway, something very new and something very different for the submariners. The commanders of *B-9* and *B-10* were long-faced, but they had been forced to agree that it was doubtful, given the condition of their batteries, if they could run for ten hours submerged, which was the estimated time for this particular mission.

At four o'clock in the morning the mission was under way. At four-fifteen Lieutenant Holbrook was guiding the submarine on the surface, three miles from the entrance to the Straits. As every night, the Turkish searchlights were sweeping the waterway in the darkness. Lieutenant Holbrook submerged and settled down to wait for dawn and the end of the spearing beams. Then it began to get light and, cautiously, checking by periscope, the Lieutenant brought the submarine to the surface and moved very slowly and cautiously to a position about a mile from Cape Helles. He gave the order: trim for diving. They were getting ready to go in.

Lieutenant Sidney T. Winn executed the Captain's orders and passed the word for diving. All during the mission, First Officer Winn would be at his captain's side, ready for any assignment.

The diving operation was done by Petty Officer William C. Milsom, a member of a spare submarine crew who had virtually forced himself on this mission. He had volunteered in such a manner that Holbrook and Winn had felt bound to accept his services. Now he was to show his value as an expert and as a man – for nine hours he would operate the diving-wheel without relief.

It was 8.22 on that Sunday morning when the submarine finally dived, and Holbrook took her down to sixty feet, then began to crawl forward in the direction of Chanak. Five minutes later the boat was at periscope depth, and he was peering about the horizon. Five seconds up, down periscope – up again and another look, and then down again.

They went down to eighty feet and began moving along at two knots against the current. They headed for the first long row of mines. All went well for half an hour, and they covered about a mile. But then there began a dreadful racket – something had worked loose or something had attached itself to the hull, and was causing a banging that Holbrook feared could be heard by every Turkish soldier on the shore. Something had to be done. Holbrook ordered the submarine to the surface, and Winn again passed the word. Petty Officer Milsom turned his diving-wheel sharply, the tanks were blown, and the little submarine headed up at a sharp angle, then levelled off so she could not porpoise out of the water and make their presence known all along both shores.

In a moment the conning-tower hatch was off and men were on deck, rushing forward to the source of the noise. They spotted the problem. The port forward hydroplane guard just installed by the mechanics of *Blenheim* had struck something and twisted around so that it was in the shape of a hook, the point banging against the hull. Two strong submariners moved forward, wrenched the useless guard free from its fittings and hurled it over the side. In less than a minute they were back inside the 'pig-boat', and the conning-tower hatch was clanging behind the commander as he saw them

43

all down. He had watched the shore anxiously during the manœuvre, fearful lest they be discovered by this unplanned surfacing. But there was no sign of unusual activity ashore. Lieutenant Holbrook once more ordered the submarine down, and she slid beneath the grey-green water, to move forward towards the inner passage once again.

It was a tricky business, negotiating the minefields. But soon they were through the first row, and then the second, and the third. By 9.40 that morning they had cleared the fifth mine sowing, and when Holbrook ordered the boat up and peered around through the periscope, he saw that he was not far from a large warship with two funnels, flying the Turkish crescent ensign at the mainmast. He sighted carefully through the periscope and took a good long look. She was off his starboard beam, anchored, settled in like an ageing maiden lady at a sewing-party.

Now to attack. Lieutenant Holbrook ordered the submarine swung around to starboard. It was a very tricky operation against the heavy current. On the way in, he and his men had a hard time keeping the boat down to depth. It took three hundred revolutions on two battery-operated electrical engines to keep her down at sixty feet, and then sometimes because of the current and water layers, she came up to forty feet without any move on the helm. On that first surfacing, Holbrook had ordered five hundred revolutions on both engines and full rise on the helm – and still it had taken a quarter of an hour to get up from twenty feet to the fifteen-foot periscope depth. Now, the movement around to come half athwart the current, yet not lose place, was difficult indeed. It took all the skill of the operators.

'Eight points to starboard,' called the Lieutenant, and the quartermaster swung the wheel.

Just then there was a dreadful sinking sensation. The submarine dropped like a stone to eighty feet. She stayed there.

The Lieutenant ordered the boat brought up, but Milsom's alterations of the diving planes did nothing. Nor did backing and filling on both engines seem to help. Holbrook sent men forward and then aft. They rocked the boat. Still the depth gauge stuck at that ominous figure: eighty feet. They blew the tanks. Nothing happened. Finally, Holbrook ordered two auxiliary tanks blown for a full five minutes. Slowly, the boat began to come up.

She rose, back up to periscope depth, and Holbrook took a new sighting through the slender instrument. He dived again, but the boat went too deep and had to be brought back up for correction. This was the difficult water, and by this time Lieutenant Holbrook was convinced that the change in the tides here was responsible for his trouble. It was that, of course, and also the undeveloped state of the art of submarine building, for by the standards of the later twentieth century the *B*-boats were primitive craft. But the men who used them knew these submarines better than any others, and they could coax those unyielding caskets of steel into most remarkable manœuvres. So it was now, with the tide running unfavourably and the boat bucking and kicking like a sea horse, that Lieutenant Holbrook prepared his attack, moving men about so that their weight in different areas would stabilize the boat.

He ordered the submarine ahead and soon reached a point about eight hundred yards off the beam of the anchored Turkish vessel. The ship was the *Messudiyeh*, and until the *Goeben* and *Breslau* had been pressed into the service of the Sublime Porte, she had been the newest and best of an ancient and doddering fleet. Still she *was* a warship, her guns *were* capable of destroying ships and killing men, and she *was* a proper target for Lieutenant Holbrook's attention.

Holbrook ordered the submarine ready. Winn sent the word that the torpedomen were to flood the tubes. That meant they were getting ready to fire. Now Holbrook did his calculations, allowing for tide and the position of the boat, and lined up on the steel side of his target.

'Stand by to fire torpedoes.'

The boat was hushed, every sound magnified in the tense atmosphere.

'Fire both,' came the order.

The torpedomen fired. The long, slender weapons rushed out of the tubes, propelled by compressed air, the valves closed behind them as they went upwards and then the motors began to run.

Holbrook stared through the periscope as the wakes showed and the torpedoes headed for the *Messudiyeh*. Suddenly he staggered and nearly fell. The submarine was caught by tide or current and swept sideways and down. The periscope disappeared from the surface. Holbrook could see nothing. The Petty Officer brought her up again, and Holbrook watched the torpedoes move along, then lost sight.

There was no mistaking the sudden thump of the starboard tube torpedo striking something. The whole boat shuddered and shook with the explosion.

Holbrook ordered the submarine back to periscope depth, and the crew struggled to do his bidding. It took a little time, and when he could see again, the *Messudiyeh* was already *in extremis*: fire was burning somewhere, and a thick greasy cloud of black smoke rose above the warship. She was down by the stern, and looked as though she might sink to the bottom.

The Turks who manned this ship were brave men. In spite of the knowledge that their ship was badly damaged they fought back. Through the periscope Lieutenant Holbrook could see flashes of flame and smoke as the Turkish gunners fired wherever they fancied they saw something dangerous. It was not long before they spotted his periscope and began coming dangerously close with their shells. It was time to move. A lucky shot and the *B-11* might well go to the bottom of the Strait forever.

Holbrook ordered the submarine to move away but kept checking the position and condition of his enemy from time to time. Only five minutes had elapsed since he had sighted the ship – only an hour and a half had elapsed since he had made that first dive to enter the forbidden waters of the Dardanelles.

The Turkish gunners continued their firing, but as the submarine moved, the danger of a hit was lighter. Then five more minutes skidded by, and suddenly the *Messudiyeh* began to move. Majestically, she turned, her upper works canting towards the horizon, as though she were bowing to the Gods. And then she turned further, the rail dipped beneath the surface, and she went all the way with a tremendous splashing, turning turtle, capsizing and sending those brave gunners and most of the crew to their deaths. Or so it seemed. Few bodies struggled in the water that day but the next day, when rescue workers cut through the upended keel of the ship and her bottom plating, they were able to rescue most of the crewmen, who had managed to survive in the air pockets of the ship.

Having seen so much, Holbrook was ready to leave those waters. By the shore, small vessels were getting up steam to give chase. A hail of fire had started from the forts that was uncomfortably close. If anyone among the English attackers of the Dardanelles had contempt for the gunnery of the Turks (or Germans, who had been training them), it would not be the crew of *B-11*. They were eager to get going and back to the safety of the squadron outside the Strait.

It was not to be easy.

Holbrook's intention was to slide down, turn the bow of the submarine towards the exit to the Dardanelles and escape swiftly under water.

So he took her down. And she hit with a sudden bump. The instruments read thirty-eight feet. They had come upon some rise in the bottom.

But there was nothing to be done. He dared not surface just there, with the commotion he had caused and the growing accuracy and activity of the shore guns. The submarine crept along the bottom in this very shallow water.

The tides or the currents were buffeting them, and Holbrook felt that they were being pushed off to the west, which meant into even shallower water.

To control the boat, Holbrook ordered her up to periscope depth, but she would not rise. Not until he ran at five hundred rpm on three engines would she respond, and then she came up so suddenly that in a moment light was streaming down into the control room through the glass portholes at the base of the conning tower. That change meant that the conning tower was sticking out of the water. What better target could the Turks ask for?

It had taken ten minutes to vent the boat and start those engines and get up only to bob like a cork. Holbrook and his men were in real danger, and the boat must be taken down.

Now, *B-11* refused to dive.

Holbrook had to re-flood those auxiliary tanks he had blown previously, and only then would the submarine respond. She was a cranky lady, no doubt about that.

Now it must be back to the bottom – for there was nowhere else to go. The damnable current had carried them westward, in Sari Siglar Bay, the broad expanse they would reach just before the Narrows if they tried to go clear through – and the charts showed how shallow was this water of the bay. So Lieutenant Holbrook must get them back out to the centre of the passage and deep water.

At this point came a new problem. Lieutenant Winn reported the compass fogged up and out of order. No repairs could be made under water. The compasses of these ancient *B*-boats were located on the deck of the submarine and were visible through a complex system of lenses. In the changes of temperature of the recent dives, the compass lenses had fogged and there was absolutely nothing that could be done about it. Holbrook and Winn would have to operate by dead reckoning if they were to save themselves and the crew of the submarine.

The *B-11* was bumping along the bottom in a fashion

never anticipated by her designers or any flotilla exercises. Luckily the bottom was layered in mud, and no sharp projectiles threatened the pressure hull. They were not exactly under water – the Turkish shells were exploding around them and might make a lucky hit at almost any time. Yet there was only one thing to do – push out. Ordering all possible speed, Holbrook stood calmly in his control room, directing his men to move that boat off the mudbank, and into the deeper water.

She creaked and groaned. Men were sent rushing forward and back to change the weight of the hull and avoid the dread suction that could stick the boat down tight.

And then *B-11* slid off her mudbank.

Holbrook moved up into the conning tower, which was still well above water. He peered through the round portholes and got his bearings. He then began issuing orders and conned the submarine out into the deeper water, until half an hour later when they were in the channel and could dive.

In deep water, *B-11* stopped as though to rest. After a time, when he hoped the Turkish shore batteries would have given up, on seeing nothing at which to shoot, Holbrook cautiously came up to periscope depth and turned the lens around this way and that. Then the submarine dived again and proceeded back up the channel to the entrance to the Dardanelles. An hour later a cautious appraisal indicated that they had come out of the Straits and were safe, so the boat was brought to the surface, and the conning-tower hatch was thrown open. They had been down for nine hours, a length of time almost unheard of in a *B*-boat. So poisonous was the air inside the steel hull that it took a half an hour to drive out the carbon monoxide and other gases and get enough oxygen inside the after section of the submarine to start up the petrol-burning engines.

The engines sputtered and coughed, and then came to life, and *B-11* headed back for the *Hindu Kush* and the safety of the base. A destroyer came up and escorted her back.

49

5 The Waiting Game

The exploit of Lieutenant Holbrook and the crew of *B-11* was the best news yet to come out of the campaign against the Turks, and it was greeted enthusiastically by the squadron and the allied world. When *B-11* came moving in to her base, the men of the squadron lined the rails of their vessels and cheered her, having already heard the news of the sinking of an enemy warship.

If Lieutenant Commander Pownall was disappointed, he did not show any chagrin. He put the works in motion to secure decorations for them all, as did Admiral Carden when the report was made to him. England was badly in need of heroes that December of 1914, and when the exploit was suddenly splashed across the newspapers of London, it created a furore. The Lords of the Admiralty, Winston Churchill leading, decided that Lieutenant Holbrook should have the Victoria Cross, Britain's highest decoration, for his gallantry. Winn was only slightly less honoured with the Distinguished Service Order, and after a little more consideration, every man aboard the boat was given the Distinguished Service Cross as well. In response to letters in the Press, a fund of £300 was subscribed for the crew, while Holbrook's old commander, Admiral Keyes, presented the captain of *B-11* with a silver tankard, inscribed with Holbrook's name and that of the *Messudiyeh*.

Admiral Carden wanted more submarines and especially some of the modern *E*-class, which were almost three times the size of the *B*-boats. But Churchill said no – the *E*-class submarines were needed in the waters around Great Britain and could not at that moment be sent out to the Dardanelles.

So it was the *B*-boats or nothing. And the fact was that the *B*-boats were in use already. The very day after *B-11*'s exploit, the commander of *B-9* took his submarine inside the Straits for an attempt at another vessel. But *B-9* was quickly discovered by the Turks and their German experts, and shells and mines began exploding around her so close by that she turned about and escaped while the going was good. It would take a little time for the heat generated by the destruction of the *Messudiyeh* to dissipate.

Lieutenant Warburton and his men were lucky to get away unscathed in their little boat.

There were more attempts, more planning and more work for the submarines. But, for the moment, the Dardanelles campaign was relatively stagnant and would remain that way until the Admiralty and the War Office decided precisely what they wanted to do about the war in that part of the world.

Meanwhile, the Germans and the Turks were anything but idle. Admiral von Usedom brought in every bit of equipment and every man that his government would spare him from Berlin, and by the end of December, the Admiral was able to report from Constantinople that the standard of Turkish gunnery was remarkably improved. He composed a detailed report about the state of the Turkish guns. Quite obviously – at least to the Germans – the British and their French allies would make some attempt to pass the Dardanelles. Why not? Given the previous state of the Turkish defences, even the Greek Navy might have been able to manage – for at the end of 1914 von Usedom calculated that the British could run the passage successfully and knock out the forts, if they were prepared to sacrifice four or five ships. The Admiral called for more guns, more weapons, more training. His plea was heard, and bigger, better and newer guns began to arrive from the west. He asked for and received torpedo tubes to be installed in the narrows in the middle of the passage. Those tubes, manned by experts, would be an excellent deterrent – more stable and accurate to fire than the torpedo tubes on any vessel.

Yet the defences were not given all the attention they should have received, because of a sharp difference of opinion between the major German 'advisers'. Von Usedom favoured a strong and immediate defence against the potentiality of the enemy. General Liman von Sanders tended to disagree with his naval advisers, holding that the British could never do much in the area without the presence of a strong land military force to back up any fleet activity. An Allied fleet arriving by itself at Constantinople could never take the city of Constantinople, and as long as the Turks held the Dardanelles, what difference would it make if half a dozen vessels managed to force their way past the defences, through the Sea of Marmara and into the Black Sea? They could never get supplies past the Turkish gunners in the Straits. They would run out of ammunition soon enough, and the Russians would not be able to supply them with the proper war materials.

Von Sanders did take some action. He reinforced the area between San Stefano and Seraglio Point at Constantinople, and he stationed extra troops in the city. He brought new army guns to the Asiatic side of the Straits' opening. He assigned several units of troops to be on watch, with reserves. He also protected the Bosphorus with extra troops against a possible Russian landing. For von Sanders suspected that the British and their Russian allies might launch a joint enterprise, landing Russian troops in the north and British in the south, to link up on the Gallipoli peninsula, destroy the forts and then hold the territory. This possibility von Sanders considered much more of a danger than an unsupported naval operation.

For several years, the Turks had been building and holding forts and trench lines against a possible Greek landing – not surprising, seeing that Greece was the natural enemy of Turkey. The trenches on the western slopes of the Kilid Bahr plateau dominated the Inner Defences of the Dardanelles. In December 1914 the defences were not adequate to withstand much of an attack by land – but that was not important at the time. The Allies had no forces with which they might attack by land. And in their councils in the early months of the war, British military and naval men alike were thinking – when they thought at all about the area – of a combined operation as the most sensible approach.

They knew something of the defences. They knew that von Sanders' strategy was concentrated against the combined attack. They knew that the Turkish forces suffered from a divided command – that no fewer than three commanders were concerned with the defences of the Dardanelles.

Since before the Turks entered the war, the British High Command had considered several aspects of the campaign. There was thought for a while of using Greek troops to press the battle, since there were no other troops available. And when the British War Council was formed that autumn of 1914, at its first meeting the question of the Dardanelles was asked again. Winston Churchill did then succeed in persuading his other council members to do a little planning for the future – collect transport ships at ports in the Mediterranean and give thought to the day when the Turkish communications along the eastern bank should be cut.

The Holbrook adventure certainly had its effects in London, where the newspapers were full of the story. But the Allies had just enjoyed a considerable success at the battle of Ypres-Yser and were considering advances on the Western Front which would demand the utmost of resources and energy. The French, in particular, seemed to believe that the tide had turned and wanted to drive the Germans from their territory with as little help as possible from the British. The belief was premature. In December 1914 the Allies were bogged down in a series of stalls and reverses, and some new thinking had to be done.

And so, in December, some on the War Council began to consider the possibility of a new front, and the Council Secretary, Lieutenant Colonel Maurice Hankey, prepared a working paper suggesting an attack on the Dardanelles and the capture of Constantinople. Not only would this move destroy the Turkish forces but it would reopen the Black Sea and return to the Allies 350,000 tons of ships that were locked up in the Danube and Black Sea ports.

As Chancellor of the Exchequer Lloyd George pointed out at about the same time, British forces would soon be augmented by half a million men who were in training. Lloyd George believed that they should not be used on the Western Front but should be put into service elsewhere, to take the pressure off that front and shorten the war. Of course it would take several months to bring an army into being, transport it, supply the forces and land them in a position to fight.

The end of December brought another factor into play that was to have an important part in the decision of the British government regarding the Dardanelles. In the week that began on Sunday, 27 December, the Turks in the Caucasus began an offensive that seemed very dangerous to the southern Russian front. Grand Duke Nicholas, the Russian Commander-in-Chief, had not believed in the danger and had refused the commander of the Caucasus front the reinforcements he wanted. Could the British do something to ease the pressure in the south?

The fact was that the Turkish offensive never developed. The Turks attacked at Sarikamish with a well-trained, strong force of men. But they were met courageously by the Russians, in one of the most stirring actions of the entire war on any front, fought at ten thousand feet in deep snow, with the temperature hovering around thirty degrees below zero, a blizzard developing. The Turkish supply lines broke down in the impossible conditions; for three days the Turkish force was without supply, which meant food as well as ammunition; and finally the Turks had to surrender much of their force at Sarikamish.

As historians would point out later, the battle was worth study at that moment for several reasons. First of all, it showed the undoubted valour and efficiency of a Turkish army trained by Liman von Sanders – facts not at all well known to the British who tended to underrate their Turkish enemies. Second, the battle so exhausted the Turkish resources for the moment that the pressure referred to by the Grand Duke no longer existed.

But as such events tend to work, the need was expressed in the Grand Duke's remarks and was paid attention by the British High Command just at a time when the debate began as to what use should be made of resources on land and sea that were going to become available in the next few months. The defeat of von Spee at sea and the clean up of many of the German raiders of the first wave freed dozens of Winston Churchill's ships, and the army was growing in strength and capability day after day.

And then – somehow – the British communications system failed.

The message from Grand Duke Nicholas had come *via* the British military mission in St Petersburg, as the worried Russian commander in the Caucasus had asked for help. The threat over, early in January 1915 Grand Duke Nicholas turned his attention elsewhere and never reported to the British mission that the battle of Sarikamish had ended in a rousing Russian victory.

Thus, on 3 January, when the Russians were taking thousands of prisoners in the snow, Lord Kitchener was talking to Winston Churchill about the chance of putting on some kind of naval 'show' in the Turkish theatre. Churchill had been very much impressed with the paper circulated by Lloyd George who was very much concerned with economic warfare and warned of new dangers approaching. Churchill recalled that he had wanted Gallipoli attacked at the outset of war. He had known very well that the Turks were in no position in November to put up an adequate defence; by January he was of the opinion that affairs had changed considerably. But he was still so much behind an attack in the south that he asked Prime Minister Asquith to call meetings of the War Council for several days running to decide on a course of action.

The Council did meet. The requests of the Grand Duke Nicholas for assistance were then laid out to the Government of Britain at the highest possible level, and it quickly became apparent that something was going to be done. So seriously did Kitchener regard the Russian problem that had been presented that he adopted an unusual course: he went to Churchill's office for the special reason of discussing this problem and the Navy's possible action in the Dardanelles.

Churchill was not in favour of a simple diversion. It was his opinion that this action would stir up the animals, cause von Sanders and von Usedom to devote even more Herculean attempts at shoring up the Turkish defences – and do nothing but hurt the chances of a future invasion from Egypt that would aim at knocking Turkey out of the war.

On 2 January, Lord Kitchener put it all in perspective. He simply did not have any forces to spare to take the pressure off the Russians in the Caucasus. He reiterated the vague thought that a demonstration of some kind at the Dardanelles might do something to stop the Turks from shipping troops north to the Caucasus. And Kitchener sent a telegram to Grand Duke Nicholas, promising that something would be done to divert the Turks.

It had to be the Dardanelles or Constantinople. Both Churchill and Kitchener could agree on that much, as other diversions had already been tried, without signal success. Most spectacular of these was a naval venture of 18 December against Alexandretta. The cruiser *Doris* landed a party of officers and ratings north of the city, to blow up the railroad line. The party tore up the line and stood by while a train coming down from the north was satisfactorily derailed. On 19 December the captain of *Doris* sent ashore an ultimatum, demanding the surrender of all military stores and rail supplies for destruction, or the *Doris* would stand in and bombard the city and could not be responsible for loss of life and property.

The Turks were slow to reply, so another naval party landed north of the settlement of Payas, ten miles north of Alexandretta, and undertook a second object lesson. The sailors blew up the railway bridge outside the town, destroyed the railway station and cut all the telegraph wires to the south. The ultimatum about the railway supplies in Alexandretta was repeated, and this time the Turks accepted, providing the British would lend them the explosives.

Now began what the British in London regarded as a comic opera. The captain of *Doris* was hardly going to hand over explosives to the enemy. The Turkish commander was not going to sacrifice his dignity by submitting to the directions of a junior officer. The Torpedo Lieutenant in charge of the demolition was at a loss. But the problem was solved by the Turks naming the British Lieutenant as a Turkish officer for that day only. Turkish cavalry then brought in the locomotives and supplies, the British blew them up with guncotton, and the *Doris* steamed away, her task completed.

This was war? It hardly seemed so. When the tale reached London, it was hard for officials who were engaged in a bloody and bitter struggle on the Western Front to take the news seriously. The Turks were notoriously corrupt, and Turkish civilization seemed to have deteriorated even more in the past quarter of a century. Winston Churchill found it hard to regard the Turks with the same implacability he would turn on the German foe. He half believed that a running of the Dardanelles, plus a strong threat of the capture of Constantinople, might bring about a suit for peace from the Sublime Porte. Or if not, perhaps conversations could be engendered, which might end in the separation of the Turks from the Germans and Austrians.

On 3 January there was a momentous communication from the new First Sea Lord, Lord Fisher, to Churchill in London, proposing a three-pronged assault on the Turks, by the British at Besika Bay, by the Greeks at Gallipoli and by the Bulgarians at Constantinople. Meanwhile, the British Fleet units at the Dardanelles (using only old ships) would force the Straits, destroy *Goeben*, *Breslau* and the lesser units of the fleet and clean up the enemy. The importance of this message was not that it had the slightest chance of being carried in the War Council. What it did do was give Churchill the impetus, or excuse, to begin fomenting one of his favourite ideas: the attack on the Turks. That very day Churchill sent a message to Admiral Carden:

> From First Lord.
> Do you consider the forcing of the Dardanelles by ships alone a practicable operation?
> It is assumed older battleships fitted with mine-bumpers would be used, preceded by colliers or other merchant craft as mine-bumpers and sweepers.
> Importance of results would justify severe loss.
> Let me know your views.

Carden replied that while the Dardanelles could not be 'rushed', they might be 'forced' by an extended operation with a large number of ships.

This was hardly a very enthusiastic response to Churchill's question, but Churchill had been getting other information, and in his own way had been digesting it to show him how he could do what he wanted. Lord Fisher was already saying that the advantage of taking Constantinople was overwhelming.

In this first week of January 1915, then, the British war authorities were considering very seriously the whole problem of operations in the south, and the Dardanelles effort was beginning to take on a life of its own. On 5 January the War Council discussed the matter, and enthusiasm rose for an operation as described by Admiral Carden, a forcing of the Dardanelles by old ships, with the implication that the channel could be kept open. Such a manœuvre would undoubtedly change the course of the war. All those materials locked up in Russia would become available; so would the ships. The Turkish war effort, if it continued at all, would be fragmented. Constantinople would soon be captured. And this could be done without the investment of the territory with hundreds of thousands of troops – as one plan had envisaged.

Churchill's enthusiasm was on the rise. That day he talked with several officials about the programme, and their enthusiasm added to his own. At the end of the week he found that the Chief of Staff (Admiral Oliver), the Admiral in charge of this particular theatre (Sir Henry Jackson) and the sea commander (Vice-Admiral Carden) subscribed to the theory that it was possible to force the Dardanelles by sea, with a minimal troop commitment for investiture of territory.

On 6 January Churchill was in action. He asked Admiral Carden for a detailed operational plan for the Dardanelles, including the ships he would need and the other elements of the force. Churchill had made up his mind: if nothing insurmountable came in the way, it would be done.

By 8 January, when the War Council met again, it seemed to be fairly well decided. Kitchener favoured the plan, largely because he had been assured that it did not pose him any big questions of manpower.

Three days later, Admiral Carden's plan came into Whitehall. It was clear and detailed, the work of a staff officer of marines who knew what he was doing. First, said the plan, they would reduce the defences at the entrance to the Dardanelles. Second, they would destroy the inside defences as far as Kephez. Third, they would reduce and destroy the forts at the Narrows and such installations as the torpedo tubes brought in by von Usedom's experts. They would

59

sweep the minefield and destroy the mines, clearing the passage for the future.

The plan would require twelve battleships, three battle cruisers, three light cruisers, one destroyer flotilla leader, sixteen destroyers, a depot ship, six submarines, four seaplanes and twelve minesweepers, plus a hospital ship, colliers and other supply vessels.

When operations began, the ships would stand off and bombard the forts, first from long range and then moving in to pinpoint targets. The torpedo tubes at the entrance to the Dardanelles would be destroyed. Then the minefields would be knocked out, and the guns commanding the field cleared away. This done, the battleships would enter the Straits, preceded by the minesweepers which would eliminate the five rows of mines that had not already been knocked out. The cruisers would reduce the forts as the battleships forced their way in. The battleships would move towards the Narrows, seaplanes would spot for them, and they would knock out the forts one by one as they went. The minesweepers would come up, sweep the mines at the Narrows and fall back, while the battleships smashed the forts at Nagara. Once again the minesweepers would move into the lead and proceed to the Sea of Marmara followed by the battleships. The breakthrough would be complete.

The big danger was *Goeben*. If she assisted the defence beyond the Narrows, there might be trouble. The answer would be to bring up modern battle cruisers to fight her if necessary. That matter would have to be decided during the course of events.

And how long would all this take? The planners had considered that, as well as most other eventualities they could foresee. Much depended on the morale of the defenders, but it might take about a month to complete the breakthrough to the Sea of Marmara. Then, two battle cruisers would stay in the Sea of Marmara, proof against *Goeben* and *Breslau* if they should not be fought in the action. Also the force in the

Sea of Marmara would include four battleships, three light cruisers, a dozen destroyers, three submarines and several minesweepers and supply vessels as needed. The remainder of the force assigned would roam the Straits, guarding against land attack, mine-laying and attack by German *U*-Boats.

As plans went, it was remarkable for its conciseness and the thoroughness of the detail. As Winston Churchill put it, 'This plan produced a great impression upon every one who saw it.'

It seemed to be the decisive factor, perhaps, because the leaders of the British war effort had already persuaded themselves that this move into the south was advantageous. All they had needed was an assurance that it could be done.

6   Can Ships Fight Forts?

In retrospect it all seems so simple.

All anyone at the upper levels of the British defence effort had to do was say 'This is impossible', and all those thoughtful, concerned leaders might have turned about and regarded the Dardanelles operation with a jaundiced eye.

But nobody questioned. Admiral Sir Henry Jackson's comments on the operation and his situation indicated more or less what was happening. Sir Henry had been consulted on the Dardanelles operation once in an offhand way one day by Winston Churchill. Sir Henry actually had very little to do with that kind of planning. His field was the Committee of Imperial Defence against the German colonies and overseas wireless stations. Churchill asked Jackson to write an appreciation of the Dardanelles idea and he did so. Although the fleet could inflict grave damage on Constantinople, he said, the situation would be in doubt unless there was a large military force to occupy the town immediately. The capture of Constantinople would be most valuable and worth considerable loss, but still many troops were needed. That was really Jackson's last basic connection with the affair. His word was used in support, as he turned his attention to the details of his own field.

And so it went. Enthusiasm was growing wherever the plan was discussed. It was all so simple. And no one said 'Look here, ships cannot capture and hold forts.' No one poured on cold water. Right up to the Prime Minister's level, the enthusiasm seemed boundless. From hindsight, the Dardanelles plan can be regarded as a matter of hypnotic influence, each man convincing himself that what he wanted to do could be done. In the highest reaches of the Admiralty, particularly, the plan was accepted.

Then someone on the War Staff suggested that the new super battleship *Queen Elizabeth* could be used in this operation with minimal danger to herself. She was scheduled to go off into the Mediterranean for gunnery trials. But why not try her and the new big guns against the Dardanelles forts? She could stand offshore, out of the range of the enemy, and calibrate her guns while reducing the Turkish installations. So simple and useful did this approach to the wasteful matter of gunnery trials in wartime appear, that it appealed to all senior officers approached. As Winston Churchill put it, 'We all felt ourselves in the presence of a new fact.'

Again, the case for the Dardanelles effort was building.

The whole, as it built, could be called a case study in the effects of power and decision in wartime. A call from Russia represented a need. The leading war officers desperately wanted to create a front in the Mediterranean for several reasons. A well-considered and apparently effective plan was presented to them. They could use their newest and most powerful naval weapon with virtually no danger.

Nagging doubts still assailed Winston Churchill and the other senior officers, for what they now advocated contravened the naval doctrine of the past few years. Since the 1880s the doctrine had held that the increased cost of building ironclad ships, the improvement in artillery, the development of the torpedo and the mine, had reversed the odds of ships fighting forts. Indeed, even in the days of sail there had been some who judiciously refrained from engaging forts, on the principle that a six-gun fort could usually hold off a ship of the line with its eighty to a hundred guns. The concepts of naval and shore defences in the early 1900s bore out that reversal of even slight chance of the ships' superiority doctrine.

But in even more recent years, matters had changed again.

The ships about which Winston Churchill was talking were old ships. They were scheduled to be scrapped during the next few years as the radically modified and much more heavily gunned battle forces emerged from the shipyards. Even so, these old battleships and cruisers on which the Navy was depending for the Dardanelles operation were superior in gunpower and range to the fortifications at the Dardanelles.

The new fifteen-inch guns were in many ways untried outside laboratory conditions, and a great deal was hoped for them as 'super weapons'. German heavy howitzers had proved their capacity of smashing modern fortifications in the land campaign of the Western Front, and this development was not unnoticed by the naval authorities. How heavy land howitzers related to fifteen-inch naval guns remained to be seen, but the optimism was certainly there, and it was shared by many of those around Mr Churchill. Sir Arthur Wilson, one of Churchill's gunnery experts, was quite sure that the fifteen-inch guns could do the job against the Turkish forts, even though fifteen-inch ammunition was as yet limited to powder-filled shells that had only about two-thirds the explosive charge of the howitzer. Technical discussion this – but it was carried out and considered along with all the other factors.

In the final analysis, the political factors turned out to be supreme, and it must be said that all else was weighted by them, for the situation of Russia was seen as growing ever more desperate because of her forced isolation from her allies. Serbia in these weeks seemed about to be conquered entirely. Greece and Rumania would like to join the Allies but were afraid to do so at that moment because they did not know what Bulgaria would do, and Bulgaria was tending towards the Germans and Austrians because they were winning so many battles.

In other words, what the Allies needed desperately at the moment in the political field was a military victory of note, not simply the destruction of a warship or two. Such a victory at the Dardanelles could mean a revolution in Constantinople, or a reversal of the German influence and a suit for peace by the Turks. The change would most certainly keep Bulgaria, Greece, Rumania and Italy from joining the Central Powers. It might persuade them to join the Allies. The freeing of the Danube ports, the opening of the Black Sea and the possibility of surrounding Austria and Germany were so appealing that they made the risk seem very attractive.

So Winston Churchill presented the idea and the Carden plan at the meeting of the War Council on 13 January. In the discussion it was agreed that, even if the effort failed, little harm would be done because the bombardment of the Dardanelles could be broken off by *Queen Elizabeth*, and she could steam away without damage.

As the findings of the Dardanelles commission were later to indicate, the vigorous personality of Winston Churchill played a key role in this meeting. Prime Minister Asquith heard the plan and the arguments and gave what he thought was a conditional approval to the Navy for operational arrangements. Obviously the Prime Minister did not understand the procedures involved, nor did others at the meeting who believed that they were only endorsing provisional arrangements. But before the meeting ended, the Admiralty was ordered to prepare for an expedition of naval forces to Turkey in February, to bombard and seize the Gallipoli peninsula and to take Constantinople. The decision was unanimous.

When the meeting of the War Council ended that day, Winston Churchill went back to his room and sent a message to Admiral Carden, telling him that the plan had been approved and that the force would be ready by 15 February. Carden was to knock out the forts one by one, as the Germans had done at Antwerp with their big howitzers. And Vice-Admiral J.M. de Robeck would be Carden's second-in-command for the operation. Carden was instructed to keep on with his work-up of the details.

How complete the commitment to the Dardanelles operation had become in those few days was shown by Churchill's action next day, when he rejected the idea of an attack in the Adriatic against the Austrians. The idea had been propounded at the War Council meeting, with the thought that an attack on the Austrian base at Cattaro would influence the Italians into either coming into the war on the Allied side or at least not joining the Central Powers. Churchill was adamant; the whole British force available for such excursions was going to be tied up in the Dardanelles operation.

'I had now become deeply interested in the enterprise . . .' wrote the First Lord of the Admiralty. And as was usual with him when he had committed himself, Churchill turned his bulldog chin up and would listen to no further arguments against the theory.

There were virtually none. Sir Henry Jackson, who might have objected had he been at the right place at the right time, was ill. No time was to be lost, so his staff were called into play to get the ships. Perhaps, had Jackson been available at the crucial moment, he would not have objected. Later he was to say that he had agreed to the attack on the outer forts but that he thought an attempt by the fleet to run the Dardanelles without an army would be 'a mad thing to do'. But would he have said that? He indicated he would not, for later on this Admiral remarked that it was not the duty of a naval man to interfere with naval policy unless asked by a superior officer for an opinion. His duty was to carry out policy. And as for the asking – why, Admiral Jackson was in bed at the propitious moment, when the politicians were asking the questions at the War Council meeting.

The messages began going out. The Chief of Naval Staff in London was ordered to begin the concentration of the fleet units that would be required for the Dardanelles move, which was now designated 'Operation Pola'. An island base had to be found. A landing-place for airplanes must be arranged at Tenedos, because Carden had specifically referred to the

November bombardment's difficulties and the need for air spotters for the artillery aboard the naval vessels. In this coming operation, where pinpoint strikes might mean everything, there should be no possibility of slip-up by failure to attend to such detail. The army had developed some new techniques of artillery spotting, using the fragile fabric and chemical-coated aircraft of the day. Churchill, with his indefatigable attention to military detail, was aware of the outlines and instructed his inferiors to get all the material available and find some planes that could be adapted to this spotter method. Furthermore, the carrier *Ark Royal* should be held for the Dardanelles operation, with eight seaplanes and airplanes.

More submarines were to be sent, including at least one of the *E*-class boats that Admiral Carden and Lieutenant Commander Pownall had been talking about. Carden was to have everything within reason that he had requested. It went into the works on 13 January.

Meanwhile, sick or not, Admiral Sir Henry Jackson was studying the detail of the plans his superiors had now embarked upon with such enthusiasm. His task was to remind the men of operations of the conditions and dangers they faced, such as the need for constant reconnaissance, the warning to remain outside the thirteen-thousand-yard range of the outer fort guns until those guns were reduced, the need to use the airplanes frequently and effectively, and the necessity of watching for mines. But, given all these cautions, the Admiral was serene about the prospects of reducing the outer forts of the Dardanelles (and that was his sole concern of the moment). They could learn as they went along, without much danger.

By the time Churchill had Sir Henry Jackson's report, even had that Admiral argued, it would have been too late. The Pola plan was in the naval machinery, and to withdraw at this moment without some specific argument that involved a change of situation would hardly have been possible. The

Royal Navy was committed, with every hope that the operation would do all that was expected.

Churchill's next move was to get in touch with the French, whose services were not so much required as requested, in the furtherance of the Grand Alliance. Briefly, the First Lord of the Admiralty laid out the plan for the French. He went further: he suggested that once they entered the Sea of Marmara, it would be essential to fight the 'Turco-German fleet immediately'. That being the case, the French were asked if they could assign a squadron of battleships, along with submarines and destroyers and the seaplane ship *Foudre*, to serve under their own rear-admiral with the British.

The commitment was made to the world in this letter. Churchill gave it every authority; he secured the signatures of the Prime Minister, Lord Kitchener and various other high officials, to show that the plan was regarded as important in the highest reaches of the British Government and would have total support of the War Council. And then, Churchill sent a similar communication to the Grand Duke Nicholas, with the suggestion that the Russians might, at the propitious moment, launch an attack on the Bosphorus. The moment would come when the outer forts of the Dardanelles were destroyed. And then, as Admiral Souchon and General von Sanders rushed their forces to protect against the British and French in the south, the Russian attack on the north would seal the doom of the Turkish war effort.

'. . . It is our intention', wrote Churchill, 'to press the matter to a conclusion, and at the right moment the intervention of the Russian Fleet will be most desirable.'

One could almost see *Goeben* and *Breslau* and those lesser Turkish vessels going up in smoke, as Constantinople burned, and the Turks, in despair, booted out the Germans and sued for peace.

Feverishly, the preparations moved ahead. The tone of Winston Churchill's correspondence allowed for no sloth. The attack on the Dardanelles should begin as soon as *Queen Elizabeth* could arrive, he said. He wanted her under way soon, for he hoped to begin the Dardanelles operation on 15 February.

In spite of the expressed optimism of the political and major military leaders, Churchill knew the politics of war well enough to set aside a certain reserve for failure. 'As soon as the attack on the Dardanelles has begun, the seizure of Alexandretta should take place. Thus, if we cannot make headway at the Dardanelles, we can pretend that it is only a demonstration, the object of which was to cover the seizure of Alexandretta. . . .'

Churchill's announced reason for this cautious preparatory byplay was the 'oriental point of view', but he was a better politician than that. He knew very well that if the Dardanelles operation failed spectacularly, the results could be as desperate to the people involved as had been the escape of *Goeben* and *Breslau* at the opening of the war. At least two fine naval careers had been ruined and another high officer had sacrificed his life needlessly, all on the altar of naval success. If the forts at the entrance were knocked out and the Dardanelles attackers saw they could go no further, the covering story could prevent embarrassment that might cause disruption in the War Council or hurt Carden and his senior officers.

That disciplined and thorough officer Sir Henry Jackson was to monitor the operation, and 'the beginning' was really right then. Admiral Carden was told that he might take his flagship *Indefatigable* to Malta for any refit necessary, while *Inflexible* took her place outside the Dardanelles. Rear-Admiral de Robeck was assigned and told to raise his flag in one of the battleships bound for the Dardanelles and go there straight away to assist Admiral Carden.

Five days after committing the Royal Navy and His Majesty's Government to the task, Churchill wrote to Lord Kitchener urging caution in the public realm. Until the bombardment was done, they could not tell how things would go and must avoid the appearances of rebuff. So the fleet would be spread across the eastern end of the Mediterranean, giving the appearance of an operation that could be centred just about anywhere – with special attention to Alexandretta, if that needed to be the bluff point.

And as the affair progressed, others added little bits and pieces to it. Admiral Fisher suggested that as long as they were going so far, why not put in the two powerful vessels *Lord Nelson* and *Agamemnon*, two of the newest of the big ships of the British Royal Navy. Like *Queen Elizabeth*, they need not really be risked but could feel their way to success or break off the action and pretend that their commitment was extremely limited.

Winston Churchill was here showing the elements of character that would dominate him during two great wars – an innovative mind that probed and questioned and seized upon opportunity or tried to make that opportunity if none existed, an imagination that soared to the greatest heights of man, a demand upon others to perform beyond their depths and to standards unimagined by history, the stubborn will to carry forth his plans, buttressed by whatever safeguards presented themselves, and the conviction that whatever he did might succeed.

All these were the elements of the coming drive against the Dardanelles that was to be 'a simple little naval operation', taking the pressure off Russia and driving with some ease a relatively minor enemy from the European war.

7 Bravery

At the Dardanelles, the excitement of the moment began sweeping through the squadron when Royal Marine Captain Godfrey completed the drawing of the plan requested by the First Lord of the Admiralty. So important a matter could hardly be kept secret in the squadron, and the feeling that something was soon going to happen began to permeate the ships and shore installations. Even before the plan was accepted, in the submarine units and the blockading ships it was suspected that there was no more question of 'blockade' – the attack would soon begin.

Quite aside from that, the French were eager to make a mark with their submarines, and Lieutenant Commander Pownall had promised them the chance, once *B-11* had made her heroic voyage, and *B-9* had suffered sad failure in her brave attempt. The French were having the same problems that the *B*-boats suffered. The French Navy had sent a number of submarines to the area, in response to Churchill's wishes, and in mid-January they were present: *Bernouilli, Faraday, Jouie, Coulomb, Le Verrier* and *Circ*. These submarines had been operating in the Mediterranean and the Adriatic, but when they arrived at the strangely different waters of Turkey, they had troubles. The currents again told the tale: the captains of the French submarines went out on exploratory missions, and returned to tell of buffetings and stoppages quite unknown to them in normal operations. Under water, their power might suddenly fail or seem to do so. They could not dive or recover as quickly as they were used to doing. They were forever at the mercy of the current that ran so swiftly from the Sea of Marmara through the rushing waterway of the Dardanelles, to empty itself in the Aegean.

Testing, trying and making ready for an operation, the French submarines faced worse difficulties than the *B*-boats; they estimated that the length of the Dardanelles should be traversable in seven hours under normal conditions. But because of the currents that had so bedevilled *B-11*, the French submarines figured that it would take them at least fifteen hours to make that passage, and their boats were scarcely equipped for it.

Still, every day one or the other of the French submarines was out on duty, penetrating the entrance to the Strait and remaining on station under water from dawn until sundown, surfacing only when necessary to clear the foul air from the inside hull of the submersible. From time to time these French submarines began to stalk one of the gunboats or destroyers that emerged from the Turkish end of the Straits. The purpose of the Turkish excursions was to check the mines and make sure that no enemy vessels were planning an attack. They also fired on the minesweepers and kept them at their distance. The French would very much have liked to attack, but the small, fast vessels made bad targets, and so day after day passed without there being much action.

Then, from Bizerte up to the Dardanelles came another French submarine, the *Saphir*, which was commanded by Lieutenant de Vaisseau Henri Fournier. He insisted that with this model submarine, he could travel 140 miles under water at five knots, which meant that he could make the passage very easily through the Dardanelles and might even be able to get a shot at *Goeben*, in the Sea of Marmara.

At six o'clock on the morning of 15 January, Fournier and his crew set out from the submarine station, bound for the passage inside. At 7.20 the submarine dived and went down to about seventy feet, in order to pass the first line of mines.

Not long after diving, the pressure hull began to take water, and the chief of the boat soon announced to Lieutenant Fournier that a rivet had failed in a spot that was impossible to repair under water. Fournier ordered the pumps started but decided to continue the mission. Slowly, the water mounted in the boat, the pumps labouring, the water not dangerous but enough to remind the submariners of the perils of the sea.

At 8.30, the *Saphir* had been under for an hour and ten minutes. The air in the boat was becoming stale, and the water leaking through the torn rivet hole was a constant irritation. But Fournier pushed on. If his British allies could do it, he too could force the Strait and bring home a victory for France. There had been too little glory so far in the Republic's war at sea.

In the middle of the minefield, they suddenly heard the scrape of a steel cable across the hull. It was enough to make a man sweat, if he were not sweating already in the dank half-darkness, the condensation running down the inner sides of the pressure hull, the lights flickering occasionally as the batteries strained at their task of powering and lighting the ship. It would not have been easy to turn about now. Nor was the idea in Fournier's mind. He gave his attention to the instruments and made his constant run of calculations about drift, position and movement ahead. He was attacking, not manœuvring, not reconnoitring.

Scrape – to Fournier's ears came the rasping of the cable of the first mine and almost immediately afterwards the scratching and screeching of a second. There was danger here. If they had been too high in the water, or if their angle of approach had dragged the cable too far, they might have touched the mine itself and almost certainly exploded one. That would have been the end of any submarine.

Saphir now slid through the first minefield. When Lieutenant Fournier was certain the danger was well behind them, he decided to take the boat up for a look through the periscope. As cautiously as the primitive diving equipment would allow, the Chief brought the boat up and levelled off at periscope depth, so that the Lieutenant might take a look about them and make his next decision.

He was on the wrong side of the minefield! One of those mine cables he had scraped, or the current, or a combination of them, had turned the little craft completely about, and he was now heading back towards the Allied base.

This would never do. Checking the compass (which, like *B-11*'s, was mounted outside the hull and was of very little use under water), Lieutenant Fournier ordered the periscope down and a turn of 180 degrees. He could have surfaced, but the motion and the splashing about would most certainly have drawn unwelcome attention to the submarine. Stealth was a major weapon, and by stealth he might succeed.

Soon the submarine was moving once more through the minefield, and this time Fournier relied on an emergency compass, one not nearly so sensitive as the boat's main compass but one that seemed to work. All went well for a few minutes. Then *Saphir* struck one of those coldwater currents that had bothered Lieutenant Holbrook so much on *B-11*'s famous journey. The boat was moving along just under thirty feet below the surface when the cold stream hit. Like a cork *Saphir*'s bow shot up at an angle of thirty-five degrees, and her prow broke water. She plunged upwards like a giant whale, streaming foam and brine from the vents, splashing and grampusing – in full view of the enemy shore. The critical angle of the *Saphir*-class submarine was fifty degrees. That is, if the hull achieved a fifty-one-degree angle from the horizontal, the liquid in the batteries would overflow into the scuppers and discharge a stream of deadly chlorine gas into the interior of the boat. This was a constant danger in submarines – an occupational hazard, one might say – but under normal operating conditions there was no reason for a submarine to achieve any such radical angle. Or so the submariners of the Allied world believed until they hit the Dardanelles.

Saphir's angle became critical; the batteries slopped over for just a moment; and the gas began to stream through the pressure hull, even as Lieutenant Fournier and his control-room crew struggled to right the boat and bring her back down.

They brought her back, by sheer force on the diving planes, but then she headed down at a steep angle. She plunged and kept plunging, moment after moment, with the Chief of Boat and the quartermasters wrenching at the wheels, and the Lieutenant shouting orders to attempt to level off the submarine. Back through the layer of cold water, into the increasing density of the deeper layers, the submarine slowed and finally, at nearly two hundred feet, she levelled off.

The crew was now choking on the chlorine that had permeated the whole submarine's living quarters. The rivet hole in the pressure hull was pouring through a cascade of water in the higher pressures of the deep. The pressure, indeed, threatened the whole boat's life, for she was not built to stand much more than this, and she groaned and creaked as Lieutenant Fournier and his men took every action to lighten her and bring her up to a reasonable depth.

They blew the pressure tanks with compressed air, forcing out the water that had ballasted them down. They brought the air pressure in the boat up to eighty kilogrammes. *Saphir* did not move. She seemed stuck in the narrow confines of the Dardanelles. The currents rushing above and around her seemed to press her nose down towards the mud.

Lieutenant Fournier ordered the boat turned sharply to starboard, but nothing happened. He ordered her to port, and she moved sluggishly about, but her angle did not change, and she did not move upwards as he had hoped. He sent the crew forward, to weigh down the bow, and she moved down. He sent the crew aft to break the suction and bring the bow up, and at the same time ordered full power on the electric motors that were sucking away the life-giving force that kept them moving undersea.

Now the rent in the hull where the rivet had failed was

growing larger as the pressure pushed the metal pieces apart. The joints were beginning to leak too, not just sweat, as the boat was used to doing. Rivulets of water began to appear at little air bubbles in the seams, as the pressure outside fought its way to smash into the air-pocket of the boat's hull. The bolts of the conning tower leaked water, and it came cascading down into the control room upon the heads and shoulders of the men who gave the submarine her 'brains'. One compartment forward began to flood, and to protect the rest they ordered the men back and locked the watertight doors.

Lieutenant Fournier saw that his situation was critical, very nearly desperate, and so he did the only thing he could do: he blew every tank, driving out every bit of water the submarine held in reserve. Blowing the tanks, raising the bow, giving full power, the Lieutenant finally broke the clutch of the sea, and the submarine again bobbed to the surface, her bow at an impossible angle above the water, and her stern well down. The electric motors stopped. *Saphir* seemed totally disabled.

Fournier could manipulate the periscope, and he got a look from his crazy angle. He was off Chanak, approaching the inner defences, where he wanted to be. But not in this condition. The chlorine, the depths and the water had done their grisly work. Half the men were choking and unfit for duty. The boat needed a thorough airing and half a dozen major repairs. She was in no condition to carry out an attack on the *Goeben* or even some lesser vessel of the ancient Turkish fleet. So much was evident.

Could she even escape? From the forts at Chanak and on the other side came what appeared to be the answer. Guns began firing, and splashes in the water gave grim indication of the intentions of the Turkish and German gunners. It would not be long before the gunners bracketed the French boat – her bow stuck out of the water like the trunk of a sunken tree.

But even at this extreme, one of the electric motors of the submarine came to life and gave Fournier power to open the vents, and let the compressed air escape and the sea water ballast come into the midships and forward compartments, to help drive that irrepressible bow back down beneath the surface. Soon the boat was on an even keel, and the other motors could be started. Fournier ordered a dive, and *Saphir* slowly responded as the shots splashed about her, none hitting yet. He managed to dive to forty-five feet, but she would go no lower, and he was afraid to test her, lest they all end their days at the bottom of the Strait. The chlorine and the water, and the pressure on the tender hull, had done their work. The boat was very nearly out of compressed air. Two of the engines were not working properly, and the leaks were growing by the moment even at this shallow depth.

Fournier knew he could not go on. He prepared the secret documents for destruction. They were weighted and made ready for sinking. He brought the submarine up to the surface, opened the conning-tower hatch and stepped on deck. Making sure the water was deep enough, he ordered the weighted bags thrown overboard and headed the submarine for even deeper water. Soon she was under fire again.

Lieutenant Fournier ordered a man below to bring up the flag of the Republic and watched as it was run up the rigging and flapped bravely, defying the gunners on the shore.

The *Saphir* came to within fifteen hundred yards of the Asiatic coast of the Strait, and Lieutenant Fournier saw that it was time for the last act.

'Open the seacocks,' he shouted, and the mechanics moved to do his bidding.

The submarine began to sink. One by one the men came off and began to swim towards the shore. Lieutenant Fournier waited as they stepped away into the water, one by one, until he was the last man on the boat. And then, as the submarine sank beneath his feet, flag still flying, he swam away from her, the guns of the Turks sending up geysers of water all around the sinking vessel, hitting and killing some of the men in the water.

One of the seamen had stayed back to help Lieutenant Fournier and be sure he escaped the sinking submarine. He gestured the man away and followed him, and they swam together, through the gunfire. The seaman tired and grew cold, and Fournier tried to carry him. They went down together.

Ahead, Ensign Cancel was killed by a shellburst. So were others. The Turkish patrol boats were coming up, and in ten minutes they reached the area. The guns ashore stopped shooting, and the Turks picked up the survivors: thirteen men of the crew of twenty-seven. The others had joined the *Saphir* on the bottom of the Straits.

This was a high price for glory.

8   Preparations

As the month of January moved along, it became apparent in London that the Dardanelles operation had become paramount in the thinking of Winston Churchill and some other officials. Not that they were neglecting their duty – Churchill seemed to be everywhere, worrying about tanks and gunpowder and the new *TNT* as well as the policy and political aspects of his position. But it seemed to some in authority that the politicians were expecting far too much harvest from the crop they were sowing in the Dardanelles.

Lord Fisher, the First Sea Lord, found that what he had believed to be a simple bombardment of the outer forts of the Dardanelles was something else. And indeed the operation had changed in the mind of Churchill and those who were going to put it into effect. It was becoming a full-scale invasion of Turkish waters. Such an invasion, of course, demanded by ordinary standards an invading army to mop up and support the naval force that would drive its way across the waterway, smashing the forts to smithereens.

There was a rub. After Churchill suggested so cogently that they must play the cards carefully and be prepared, if the operation failed, to suggest to the world that the whole business was a mask to cover an invasion of Alexandretta, the First Lord had a rude shock. Lord Kitchener replied to that message that he could not spare a single squad for an Alexandretta landing. The Australians had gamely sent an army to aid their English cousins in the struggle, and that army was in training in Egypt. But an army in training is not an army ready to fight a war, and Lord Kitchener was not going to send green men into battle to pull out political chestnuts.

Besides, Lord Kitchener fully expected an attack by the Turks and their allies on the Suez Canal. Suez was the British lifeline to the east, and while the Dardanelles operation was dear to Winston Churchill's heart, no one would let the Empire die from losing this vital artery to the south.

The point here is that each member of the War Council had areas of concern that so dominated his thinking that no one but Churchill was really giving the Dardanelles operation as much consideration as it should have. That was his area of responsibility, of course. Later, much later, professional navy men, along with other political and strategic critics, would criticize Churchill and sniff that such naval matters ought not to be put into the hands of politicians. But how else did a free country wage war?

One peculiarity of the British war effort lent itself to the kind of problem the Dardanelles was to present. The composition of the War Council made it a committee of the Cabinet, with naval and military experts whose function was to give advice but whose presence often seemed to lend an air of authority in military and naval matters to what were essentially still political decisions. The War Council had even more power than the old Committee of Imperial Defence, which it had replaced. It was, in effect, an oligarchy running the war. Prime Minister Asquith was chairman; Lord Kitchener, the Secretary for War and First Lord of the Admiralty Churchill were the other prime movers. Sir Edward Grey, the Foreign Secretary, attended meetings, but not always. The same was true of Lloyd George, the Chancellor of the Exchequer, and Lord Crewe, the Secretary for India. But no one contradicted the claim that the Prime Minister and the ministers responsible for the army and the navy were the ones who shaped the conduct of the war.

Although Prime Minister Asquith was chairman, it was generally held that Lord Kitchener dominated the War

Council. No one could remember a time when any desire of his was overruled by the Council or the Cabinet. Of course he was an expert, acclaimed throughout the Empire for triumphs in South Africa, India, Egypt and the Sudan. Winston Churchill was an entirely different man, with a politician's personality, and he was regarded as 'an inspired amateur' in military matters. All the way, he dreamed of a victory through the southern sea – he saw that if the Germans could be split away from Turkey, and Russia's resources opened up, the war would end very swiftly. And this vision must not be forgotten when considering the manner in which events proceeded from 1 January 1915 until the spring.

No one ever doubted that Churchill, like the others, wanted a joint military-naval operation against Turkey that winter. But the difference was that the others would never have considered anything else, while Churchill was so eager to pursue his ultimate objective that he dreamed it could be done piecemeal. Churchill was the astute observer of the military scene, his mind forever probing for new ideas, new techniques. He embraced air power, almost from its first days and, over the violent objections of his wife, decided to learn to fly. He had observed the celerity with which big German guns had demolished the Belgian forts at Liège and Namur – knocking down forts that before the war were deemed impregnable. He had been in Antwerp in October when the German guns were booming and had seen for himself. His enthusiasms were immediate and infectious, and his personality was so strong that these were easily communicated.

And yet there is another aspect of the War Council that warranted probing before the spring of 1915. There was, between politicians and military experts, a basic misunderstanding of the roles of each. The politicians invariably brought with them to the Council their military experts. Lord Kitchener did not consult his generals in the meetings – he was, of course, a general himself and functioned on two levels – as political and military expert. Obviously this

81

manner of procedure had a serious effect on the way in which the naval men comported themselves. Lord Fisher and Sir Arthur Wilson were members of Churchill's War Staff Group, and both of them attended War Council meetings, along with Sir Henry Jackson and Vice-Admiral Sir Henry Oliver. It was a formidable, highly experienced and able group of professional naval officers. Only later was it to come out that they did not regard themselves as members of the War Council group at all – and that they would not consider speaking up to disagree with the Prime Minister, the War Minister or the First Lord of the Admiralty. It was not, they said, for them to speak unless spoken to. Their job was to provide information for Churchill if he wanted it. Later they each testified that if they disagreed on any point with the politicians, they must be silent or resign.

But the members of the Council had an entirely different view of the perquisites and responsibilities of the naval men. Whenever he went to a meeting, Churchill said, he was accompanied by Lord Fisher and at least one of the others. When he spoke up for the Admiralty, he thought he was speaking the minds of his chief professional officials, as well as himself, offering ideas considered and discussed at daily staff meetings. And, Churchill added, every time he made a suggestion in the War Council, it was made before naval colleagues who 'had the right, the knowledge and the power at any moment to correct me or dissent from what I said, and who were fully cognizant of their rights'.

All the civilians connected with the War Council had the same view; had anyone in January suggested to Mr Asquith that the military and naval men were not there to advise *in camera*, he would have been shocked. But that is the way it was, as the War Council considered its multifarious and potentially disastrous decisions on every aspect of the war. Carried to its final conclusion, one could say that the generals and admirals in their own opinion had no responsibility at all for the conduct of the war in 1914 and 1915.

So as January moved to its end, here was a strange situation: from day to day Churchill brought forth elements of the Dardanelles plan. All the while Lord Fisher was instinctively against the plan, and he was certain that it must be a failure. He had said as much in the initial discussions with Churchill, before the matter went to the War Council. One problem, of course, was that the strong-minded Churchill had thought he had convinced Fisher by argument, when all he had done was silence him; it was not in the naval tradition for a junior to question his senior once he had delivered his opinions, even when asked. And no matter how grizzled an officer might become in the naval service of his country, he was always junior to the politician. Future wars would place the position of the military man higher, as the techniques of warfare became ever more complex, but in 1915 modern war as the twentieth century would know it was just beginning, and the politicians had a lot to learn.

As it happened, the naval officers never lost their objections to the manœuvre that Mr Churchill advocated, and even as they went ahead, they objected silently. And all the while, Winston Churchill thought they were with him, word and deed!

How confused it all was became certain at the end of January, as the plan was moving to fruition. The Admiralty should prepare for a naval expedition in February to bombard and take the Gallipoli Peninsula 'with Constantinople as its objective', declared the War Council in its official minutes.

One can see readily here that these busy men of the War Council were simply not thinking, once they had agreed fuzzily on the elements of the Dardanelles plan. For the key word in that sentence was 'take', and absolutely nothing was being provided with which to take Gallipoli, a long peninsula running the whole of the European side of the Dardanelles Strait. It would require 150,000 men, said the army, to take that peninsula. But there was the word in the minutes, without even an explanation.

Lord Fisher sat there, as this was done and written down, and said nothing at all. Next day he made arrangements for the big battleships *Lord Nelson* and *Agamemnon* to join the Dardanelles force. And yet, already, Lord Fisher was squirming and would soon make it plain to Winston Churchill that he did not like the Dardanelles idea. He would also write a letter to Prime Minister Asquith suggesting that the Dardanelles operation be called off!

In theory it might not be too late to stop the operation. In fact, on 25 January, when Lord Fisher wrote to the Prime Minister, it was already too late. Winston Churchill had his neck bowed; he learned quickly enough of Fisher's letter to the PM and replied immediately with a memorandum of his own, defending the plan. The basic force comprised old battleships that would soon be scrapped; Lord Fisher was over-concerned about the use of these vessels when he complained that they represented the only reserve behind the Grand Fleet.

Prime Minister Asquith put aside his other important duties long enough to invite Churchill and his First Sea Lord to the ministerial room for a private meeting before the War Council session of 28 January. They discussed the plan; the two politicians agreed that the technician's view was not broad enough, that the plan should stand, and they all went into the War Council session.

Winston Churchill pressed home the discussion of the Dardanelles plan. He was not warned (although this matter was a grave and important disappointment) by a recent message from the Russians that they could not help at all. The Grand Duke would not remove a single company operating against the Germans and Austrians to send troops south. The Russians were building battleships, but the new ones were not ready. The Russian submarines were of an old type and of no use in these waters. The Russian destroyers were not fast enough to launch an attack or to try to penetrate the Bosporus. The Russians' other ships did not have enough coal, and the winter weather in the Black Sea was too bad for coaling anyway. The Turks had too many big guns at the Bosporus, and the nearest Russian base was twenty-four hours away.

The Grand Duke would have preferred the operation to be delayed until May. The Russian Black Sea Squadron would then be reinforced by the battleship *Imperatritza Marie*, and the Russians' new submarines would be available.

It would demand the employment of two army corps simply to force the Bosporus, estimated the Russian General Staff, and they had no men to spare for the purpose. (That estimate should certainly have been a grave warning of what it would take to invest the Gallipoli peninsula.)

But if the gallant British Allies wished to continue the operation against the Turks on their own, the Grand Duke assured them that the Russians would welcome it. Such a move must have 'important results'. The operation could not crush the Turks in the Caucasus, but the action could create difficulties between the Turks and the Germans, could paralyse Turkey and could determine the attitude of the neutral states.

These results, enunciated earlier and given calm consideration, might have been enough to sway the Council against the Dardanelles operation. All that had happened had come about in response to the plea of the Russians for assistance to turn off pressure in the Caucasus. Even without direct news of the battles, the British allies should have been alerted by the tone of the Grand Duke's message. Yet Churchill was already trapped by his own imagination.

Lord Fisher squirmed. He had asked Churchill to excuse him from the War Council meeting of 28 January. In the meeting with Asquith, he had presented most of his objections but not all of them. And then they all repaired to the War Council room, for what must be the confrontation on the subject.

Churchill laid it all out. He had been in touch with the

Russians and promised them that Britain would go ahead. He had asked for, and received, French co-operation, and the French were sending vessels. Politically, Britain was certainly committed to the operation, and to withdraw from it at this point would have been embarrassing in relations with the Allies.

But objections had been raised. Did the War Council attach real importance to the Dardanelles operation (as Churchill had been given to believe)? Lord Fisher was unhappy in this situation, always conscious of the unwritten code that the service officer must not argue with the politician. But he must argue – his whole being called for argument against what he was convinced was a foolhardy errand, endangering the lives of men and the bodies of ships, and even perhaps throwing Britain's naval superiority into the balance. The battle of Dogger Bank had just ended, and it indicated that the Germans could be more than a nuisance if they decided to bring out their High Seas Fleet to fight. He understood that this question would not be raised today, said the First Sea Lord, squirming in his chair.

In view of the steps that had already been taken – the ships of reinforcement were at sea and nearly at their destination – the question could certainly not wait, said Prime Minister Asquith. Lord Kitchener chimed in. He had heard all the arguments made for the operation and he had agreed. Now he was more than forceful. The naval attack at this time was vital. If it worked, the Dardanelles operation could create the effects of a campaign with a whole army. And what were they worrying about? Much had been made of the firepower of the big ships involved. If the firing did not succeed, then all they had to do was break off the action.

The meeting had begun at 11.30 that morning. In half an hour it had taken a decidedly unpleasant turn. Tension filled the big room.

Mr Asquith attempted to heal the growing breach between the naval experts and the politicians. He pointed out once again the great expectations of the campaign. The successful attack would cut the Turkish army in two. It would capture Constantinople. It would open up Russia to exports and bring Britain badly needed wheat. It would save the Russian *rouble* in the market of international exchange, where the *rouble* was falling almost daily. It would open a passage to the Danube. It would bring Bulgaria on tc the Allied side. It would at least neutralize all the Balkans.

Asquith went further in his summary. Admiral Carden said it could be done. (He did not say *what* Admiral Carden said could be done.) It could probably be done in a month.

As such embarrassing moments are often bridged, so it was this day. The politicians covered their embarrassment by asking technical, and not very relevant, questions. Lord Haldane asked if the Turks had any submarines, and Mr Churchill said he did not think so. The bombardment would not cost much, he added, although they must be prepared for some losses in sweeping for mines. But the implication was that minesweepers were cheap.

Churchill indicated on a map what the difficulty would be. This display covered a most distressing incident. For on hearing that the Prime Minister insisted on discussing the Dardanelles project, Lord Fisher left the table and walked over to a corner of the room, apparently intent on going out. Lord Kitchener got up and followed him, seeing his old acquaintance obviously in distress.

What did Fisher intend to do? He was going to his own room where he would write out his resignation as First Sea Lord, said Fisher. All knew his position on this matter, and by the way in which it had been handled, he had been driven to open disagreement with the First Lord of the Admiralty. Under the naval code, all that was left was resignation.

Not so, said Lord Kitchener, speaking as one professional to another. The Dardanelles decision had been made by the Prime Minister himself; it was the policy of the government – Fisher had expressed his feelings, and like any midshipman he could now go back to duty and do his duty in the navy manner, as a thousand captains had done theirs before him.

When it was put on a professional basis, the pill was easier for Lord Fisher to swallow. Kitchener had shrewdly appealed to patriotism, honour and duty, qualities very high in the mind of this Sea Lord. So he went back to the table and sat down. Churchill finished his dissertation; everyone at the table seemed to be with him; and Lord Fisher was now calmly silent. So the meeting came to an end.

Churchill had observed the conversation between Kitchener and Fisher, and he now asked Fisher to come to his room after luncheon. There Winston Churchill brought out his most charming manners and persuaded the recalcitrant sea dog that he must support this Dardanelles operation with all his soul. And such was the presence of Winston Churchill that Lord Fisher was persuaded to do precisely that, against all his best judgement and his knowledge as an expert on naval warfare.

'When I finally decided to go in,' said Lord Fisher later, 'I went the whole hog, *totus porcus*.'

Churchill was perfectly satisfied. He knew he could count on the honour and character of his First Sea Lord. He knew that the enterprise was in totally sympathetic hands, now that the debris of disagreement had all been washed away.

'During the period of choice,' he said, 'a man must fight for his opinion with the utmost tenacity. But once the choice has been made, then the business must be carried through in loyal comradeship.'

That was always the navy way. That was Churchill's way, and far beyond and above the affair of the Dardanelles it would be the Churchillian philosophy.

By the end of the day, a most exasperating day, the affair of the Dardanelles was definitely settled for the first time, and the operation could continue without concern. Winston Churchill left Whitehall a serene man.

9   Of Ships and Men

Many times in the next few months, Winston Churchill was
to turn over in his mind the plan for the action at the Dardanelles, and always he came to the same conclusion: it was
perfectly sound.

To be sure, the Churchill plan was a violation of naval
doctrine that ships could not successfully attack land installations except under exceptional circumstances. But naval
doctrine must change with the times, and the war of 1914 was
bringing entirely new methods and ideas to the process of
killing. As Churchill saw that the tank was going to do away
with the horse, and the airplane was going to revolutionize
warfare in another way, so he looked upon the naval
weapons. The ships he proposed to risk at the Dardanelles
could be withdrawn at any time if the going got too difficult.
Further, four of those ships had already been condemned by
the Admiralty, and if they were not used, they would be
scrapped. Most of the others were ready to go into the
southern dockyards to be assessed: either they were ready
for scrapping, or they would be kept 'in reserve', which
meant that they would rot away without being used. So they
were expendable.

As for the men, Churchill never quite got around to
commenting on that, but in wartime soldiers and sailors *are*
expendable, and only the queasy or faint-hearted would
attempt to say anything to the contrary. Churchill's critics
might call him heartless, but they could never claim that he
was short of courage or that he would have failed to send his

own son into such a situation as the Dardanelles, had this been in keeping with duty.

The ships that he was going to use, with the exception of a handful, were of no value in fighting Germany directly. And Churchill and his admirals had already provided for the safety of the British Isles in the Grand Fleet. The Russians and Lord Kitchener held that the naval operation in the Dardanelles might shorten the war by months if not years. To Churchill that was enough; he was ready for the gamble, and he had convinced the person it was necessary to persuade, the Prime Minister.

It was, Churchill was forever to declare, a plan very certainly worth the risks involved. The French agreed. Once the details were ironed out in London, and the objections of all had been overcome, Churchill was in touch with Paris. He outlined the plan. On 2 February 1915 Monsieur Augagneur, the Minister of Marine, telegraphed his enthusiastic support: 'I have taken cognizance of the memorandum which you addressed to me on the date of 2 February. The dispositions which it contains raise no objections on my part; they seem to me united with prudence and foresight, permitting themselves to be stopped without moral damage if the continuation of the operation encounters difficulties.' So the French were with him all the way, as they had shown previously in the brave effort of the *Saphir* to torpedo the *Goeben*.

And now the armada was to proceed without fail. Instructions were sent to Admiral Carden, telling him what he would have with which to fight. First and foremost was the new supership, HMS *Queen Elizabeth*, with the fifteen-inch guns on which Winston Churchill counted for so much. How easy it would be, Churchill intimated in the orders to Carden, for *Queen Elizabeth* to stand out of range, finding the enemy with single shots. Perhaps salvoes would not be in line at all. Ammunition was so important a matter that the First Lord of the Admiralty had recently devoted a special study to the problem.

Small wonder that Churchill was impressed with this vessel. In every way she marked a revolutionary change in British naval thinking. She was the greatest thing afloat since *Tiger* and would be until the coming of *Hood*. *Queen Elizabeth* represented the building programme of 1912, and with her coming the Navy dropped the construction of battle cruisers, because this fast battleship could do the job better. She was 645 feet long overall, and with a full load she displaced 33,000 tons. She carried eight fifteen-inch guns, sixteen 6-inch guns, a pair of three-inch anti-aircraft guns to discourage snoopers, and four three-pounders. She was heavily armoured, beginning with a belt on her sides that was thirteen inches thick at some points. Barbettes, turrets, conning tower and decks were armoured, and so were torpedo bulkheads. Her engines and four screws were designed to deliver 75,000 horsepower, or twenty-four knots.

She was the first battleship to be oil-fired instead of using coal – and what a difference that made! Not for her men those long choking hours of hauling coal sacks from lighter and shore station to the deep holds. No longer would grimy sailors in stokers' undress sweat and shovel before the god of flame. It was now a matter of turning valves and watching fire-heads, of care and precision. The *Queen Elizabeth* would be clean and truly majestic in every way. Her coming changed warfare, of course, but most of all it changed the Royal Navy's engineering establishment, for herein was a true revolution.

Those guns on which Winston Churchill counted for so much were indeed powerful. They would send a 1,920-pound shell for 23,400 yards, at the rate of two a minute. The thick belt of armour at the sensitive waterline could protect her from the shots of anything afloat; even a torpedo from a deadly *U*-boat striking that armour would scarcely create an impact.

She had been three years in the building at Portsmouth Navy Yard, starting in October 1912, and was commissioned just a few days before the final decisions were made about

Dardanelles. And now she was ready to go to the Mediterranean, ready for the task settled on her.

The other ships assigned now to the operation were:

Inflexible, with twelve-inch guns
Swiftsure and *Triumph*, with ten-inch guns
Majestic and *Prince George*, with twelve-inch guns
Ocean, *Albion*, *Canopus* and *Vengeance*, with twelve-inch guns
Ark Royal, a seaplane carrier
Doris, *Amethyst*, *Sapphire*, *Dublin*, *Blenheim* and *Swanley*, destroyer depot ships
Eight destroyers of the *Beagle* class
Eight destroyers of the *River* class
One yacht to manage trawlers that would sweep for mines
Twenty-one minesweeper trawlers
Six submarines

The orders were specific as to the protection to be paid *Queen Elizabeth*. Under *no conditions* was she to be risked in this operation; she was added only because it was totally expedient to use the Turkish forts for her gunnery practice. It was important, said the Admiralty, that her guns should not be abused or in any way unduly worn, nor should any undue amount of her expensive ammunition be expended. She was not to be risked.

From London, the Dardanelles operation did not seem so very difficult. From out of range of the forts, *Queen Elizabeth* was to begin her bombardment and take on fort after fort. 'The destruction of the fort will be entailed,' said Whitehall, 'if from five to ten of *Queen Elizabeth*'s heavy shells can be dropped in it.' Carden would anchor other ships inshore so they might observe the fall of the shot and communicate corrections to the big battleship. Also, the new airplanes would be invaluable for spotting. There were not to be any salvoes, said the orders; salvo-firing against forts would be wasteful. And here Churchill went back to his observations at Antwerp of the work of the German howitzers, which had so impressed him. Those thirty-eight-centimetre howitzers which he had seen used about five rounds to find the forts' range and then another five rounds to demolish each fort. The battleship should try to do the same.

Naval gunnery experts had a tendency to read those parts of the orders twice – for what Churchill did not know was that there was vast difference between the firepower of the fifteen-inch guns and the thirty-eight-centimetre howitzers – the short-range howitzer had a far more effective explosive charge by the nature of the weapon. The guns were built for different purposes – a fact that Churchill had overlooked.

Once the forts were destroyed by the gunfire, said the orders, a base was to be seized and garrisoned. That would give the Allies their foothold for control of the Dardanelles. The entrance forts of Cape Helles and Kum Kale should be bombarded at long range from anchored vessels, and then the old battleships could move in to draw the fire of the forts and silence any remaining guns. That done, the trawlers would come in to sweep the whole area free of mines and should expect to draw fire from guns in emplacements along the shore. Bigger ships must back up the trawlers and silence those shore guns.

As the sweepers closed in, they would be brought under machine-gun and infantry rifle fire, and the support vessels would have to fire back, quietening the gun emplacements, knocking out machine-guns and the torpedo tubes that had been built up along the shore. If the torpedo tubes could not be found from the sea, then men would have to be landed, and for this purpose two battalions of Royal Marines were being dispatched to Malta. They would be garrison forces, attack forces and mop-up forces for any troop operation that was needed.

Admiral Fisher and his planning staff did the best they could for Carden and his men. Fisher said that once he had agreed to the operation, he threw his weight behind it, and this was most certainly true. They considered the problems of buoys and drift nets to catch loose mines that might be floated down on them by the enemy. They sent out submarine nets and made arrangements to establish agents of naval intelligence in the Greek islands off the Dardanelles, to watch for submarines or enemy supply vessels and to prevent the establishment of secret submarine bases. Fisher even planned a decoy squadron, to frighten the Germans and Turks. Several merchant vessels were given wood and canvas funnels and superstructures to look like battleships, and these were sent to Tenedos, where they were kept in plain sight to confuse the enemy about the British strength that was moving in for the operation.

So the Dardanelles operation moved onwards. The French began to prepare to send two battleships and several other ships to join the British. Obviously a base of supply and operations would be needed to mount the offensive, and the Greek government offered the use of Lemnos and several smaller islands in the same group. It was a neat solution; theoretically Greece was neutral in the war, but actually her whole sympathy was with Britain and against the traditional enemies in Turkey. The Lemnos group had been awarded to Greece after the Balkan wars, but the Turks had never acknowledged the Greek right to the islands. Therefore there was no violation of neutrality in the takeover, and the British could be expected to subdue the Turkish opposition on the islands and make them fit for Greek habitation at the end of the war.

All this was done by early February, with the belief that the operation would be strictly naval, that the timing would depend on the gradual reduction of one fort after another and the slow movement of the armada through the Dardanelles until finally it reached the Sea of Marmara and the inevitable engagement with the Turkish Navy.

Even as these plans were forwarded to Admiral Carden they were in a sense superseded by events. The successful British action of the naval forces fighting off Dogger Bank had allayed many fears at home about the strengths and intentions of the German High Seas Fleet. And at the same time, the chances of a British offensive on land in the Zeebrugge area were removed by the withdrawal of a huge French army from Flanders. The war on the Western Front was going to be a longer proposition than anyone had expected.

Sir John French, the British commander in France, wanted all the troops he could get, but Churchill took himself to France and argued for the Mediterranean diversion movement, and the result was that at least two divisions of troops were promised for the middle of March.

So, suddenly, by the first days of February, troops seemed to be available to make possible an entirely different kind of operation in the Dardanelles, the one regarded as most effective: a combined sea and land assault. At the War Council meeting of 9 February, the planners tried to bite off too much. They were exceedingly eager to draw the Greeks into the war and offered them two divisions of Allied troops if they would come in. But the Greeks did not believe that two divisions would be enough if the Bulgarians entered on the side of the Germans. And the Bulgarians had just made a big loan arrangement with the Germans, which did not augur well. The discussion on 9 February was not about sending troops to the Dardanelles but of opening up a whole new front at Salonika. A week was spent in negotiations with the Greeks, and it was not until 15 February that these failed and the attention of Lord Kitchener and the other military men could be brought back to the Dardanelles.

Meanwhile, Winston Churchill had not lost an iota of faith in the Dardanelles operation and was pushing it forward. Lord Fisher was beginning to cry out for divisions of troops as the apparent availability became known, for he was very worried about another grain harvest in Russia the following summer, with no way of getting the wheat to England. Churchill was very much aware of the growing chance of

95

using the troops he wanted. Assembled in Egypt and the Greek islands, the army force could march in behind the naval flotilla and seize the isthmus of Bulair, if the Turks began to evacuate the peninsula in the face of the moving bombardment ships. Or, if the Turks gave up, which seemed quite likely at that moment, then the military could occupy Constantinople; or the troops could be sent to occupy these positions after the ships had done their damage to communications and the forts. Aware of these ideas, Lord Fisher pressed his own view: the need for troops was imperative. And on 15 February, Sir Henry Jackson suggested to Admiral Carden that he did not like the naval bombardment without strong military assistance or a military follow-up. This opinion was, of course, also transmitted to Churchill and to the War Council on 16 February.

That day Prime Minister Asquith, Lord Kitchener and Churchill met with their various assistants, and discussed availabilities and needs. They decided then that the 29th Division, which was in England, could be dispatched in about ten days to Lemnos, and that another force of troops could be sent from Egypt if it seemed necessary. These troops, plus the Royal Marines already sent out, could be available to back up the naval operation if that seemed to be indicated. Some transport would be taken out with the 29th Division, and the Admiralty would begin collecting other craft in the area.

So the way was paved at last for the combined sea–land operation that the naval experts thought essential to secure the Dardanelles, once the naval bombardment of the forts had rendered the passage free and made the waterway available. Apparently bemused by Churchill's air of assurance, the others did not suggest that the naval plan should be changed and that an amphibious assault should be incorporated in an entirely new operation.

Mudros was to be the centre of it all. Rear-Admiral Wemyss was appointed to manage the naval base there, and the Admiralty began ordering up transports for the 29th Division. They would be sent to Mudros harbour on Lemnos just as soon as possible.

Or would they? The very day after Churchill had given orders, he learned that the French and a number of British officials were putting pressure on Lord Kitchener not to divert any troops from the Western Front. The whole question that Churchill had originally raised was only now becoming controversial among the 'experts'. An argument was brewing between those who favoured the 'Western' and the 'Eastern' policies. Two days later Kitchener changed his mind and said that Churchill could not have the 29th Division after all.

10   First Attempts

Kitchener came to the War Council meeting of 19 February, his erect figure showing the effects of the turmoil. Speaking slowly, he announced that he could not consent to the dispatch of the 29th Division to the east for use in the Dardanelles operation. Since they had last talked, he said, intelligence reports from Russia had indicated a growing weakness of the Allies on that front, and it was conceivable that the Germans and Austrians would begin diverting troops to the Western Front.

Churchill left that meeting disappointed but undismayed. He did not cancel the orders for transports. He noted only that the 29th Division might not be employed.

The military operations had been put in motion and they were proceeding. Two battalions of Royal Marines belonging to the Royal Naval Division received their warning orders on 29 January, and on 6 February they left Malta for Mudros on Lemnos island. Their orders were to be ready to launch landing parties and take gun positions for the fleet. But, as anyone knew, it would be another month before the main body of troops now expected to help the operation would be in the area. These things took time. All through the planning, Churchill had insisted that not even all the fleet units need be in place to begin the task of reducing the outer defences.

In retrospect it all seems odd; one cannot do more than estimate the temper of the times, and it does no good to examine the procedures of landing actions on foreign shores from the standpoint of the second half of the twentieth century. It also seemed that Lord Fisher and his contemporary professionals of the Royal Navy were so pleased at having apparently won the day in the matter of troops, that they did not wish to upset the Churchill plan any further.

There was another reason: all that Kitchener feared about collapses on the eastern front had some substance. Bulgaria was coming close to joining the Germans and Austrians, and it was believed that perhaps the first strike at the Dardanelles would give Bulgaria pause, would strengthen the pro-Allied forces in Rumania and would stiffen the Greeks so they might soon join to help the Serbs.

Further, there were persistent reports that the Peace Party in Constantinople was gaining strength – and those who liked to dream were hoping that the presence of a number of Allied ships blasting those outer defences would bring about the Turkish withdrawal from the war without a real battle. And lastly, the Turkish military was tremendously underrated by the Allies. Both military and naval planners believed it most likely that the Turks would evacuate the Gallipoli peninsula once their communications were cut to the Asiatic mainland.

While the politicians and generals argued and changed their minds, Admiral Carden prepared to go into action at the Dardanelles. The ships sent out from English and French bases began to come in and report. The French ships *Suffren*, *Bouvet* and *Gaulois* arrived, eager and ready for any action that might be indicated. Carden also planned to make use of *Queen Elizabeth* – as ordered – and *Agamemnon*, *Triumph*, *Inflexible*, *Cornwallis*, *Albion*, *Amethyst*, *Vengeance* and seven minesweeping trawlers.

It was a mixture of ships, but it was a good fleet for the task at hand. *Inflexible*, one of the first of the battle cruisers, had eight twelve-inch guns and in a way was a fine ship. But she was, in the modern sense of 1914, neither one thing nor the other. She was not sufficiently heavily protected by armour to be put in a battle line with the modern battleships. She was too big and costly to be used as a cruiser. (Her sister ship *Invincible* blew up and sank at Jutland, with the loss of a thousand men.) But for the Dardanelles she was just right. *Vengeance*, the flagship of Admiral de Robeck, the second-in-command at the coming fight, and *Albion* were sister ships; *Albion* having been commissioned in June 1901 and *Vengeance* a year later. Each carried four twelve-inch guns that would be useful in this contest. The most unusual of the vessels was the *Ark Royal*, the seaplane carrier commissioned on 9 December 1914, which carried twelve officers and 120 men, plus the air service. As for guns, it was nothing to talk about: three-pounders, Maxims and twelve-pounders for protection against small craft and other aircraft, and not much else. On 29 January she had been ordered out from Chatham to Gibraltar and had moved through heavy weather, losing several ladders overboard as testimony to the power of the sea and suffering a heavy roll all day long on 4 February. On 8 February she was in Gibraltar. Next day she was off for Malta and on 17 February she arrived alongside *Vengeance* and *Triumph* in Tenedos harbour, in sight of the Turks a few miles away.

So Admiral Carden's force was shaping up, as he issued his orders for the first action, to begin on the morning of 19 February.

As Churchill had been at so much pains to point out, the plan called for pinpoint striking. *Queen Elizabeth* was not yet in harbour, but Carden expected her up in time to work next day. Carden's flagship was very busy on 17 February, as the staff put together the orders for the next day's battle. Officers in their blues poured over maps and made calculations. Bluejackets manned the boats, and coxswains took care as they came alongside the men-of-war, bearing the orders of the day. The orders were as complete as a man could make them, including such details as instructions on washing and clean clothes to avoid septic wounds. And aboard the ships the officers received their orders and made their action plans.

There were four forts. Two stood on each side of the entrance to the Dardanelles, which, from Kum Kale on the Asian side to Sedd-el-Bahr on the European, measured just over two miles. One fort stood on the cliff at Cape Helles, just to the left of a wide beach. Another fort lay low down on the right of that beach, close to Sedd-el-Bahr, which was named in honour of the medieval castle that topped it. The famous fortification had withstood a military expedition many times, and even now, as the British prepared to attack, the remains of the past could be seen, great stone cannon balls, shot from primitive guns of a hundred years and more before, lying at the base of the stone works that had put down thousands of archers, crossbowmen and spearmen in the years since the Dardanelles had become known as the prize of Eurasia.

Those were the defences on the European side of the Strait, and for their times they had been powerful enough; but their state now represented what had happened to the Sublime Porte in nearly every way. Time had passed by the caliphate, its passage scarcely noted in the echoing halls and silken chambers of the royal palaces. The largest guns in the fort at Sedd-el-Bahr were but 10·2 inches in size, and they could not compete with the weapons the British could launch from the sea. For years the fort had sat somnolent, and now the officers of Admiral von Usedom feared they might have to pay the price of the waste and decadence of the caliph's rule over the years.

On the Asian side, those few miles across the blue water, stood the fort of Kum Kale, brisk and bold, at the very mouth of the Strait, quite close by the cliffside village of Yeni Shehr, whose janissaries and sailors over the years had manned the fortifications from time to time. These were historic spots – for the River Mendere separated these places from the plain of Troy, and these waters had borne Greek ships whose sailors had once plotted to build a great wooden horse. From walls not far away, Paris had looked down and spat upon the Greek fleet, and on those shores the beautiful Helen had once walked. The classicists among the British officers found the cool air redolent with the incense of history, even as their prosaic professional fellows armed the guns and looked to the brass of their men.

Kum Kale was not so heavily gunned a place as Sedd-el-Bahr. Only four of those ten-inch guns stood at the Asiatic bastion, with a handful of smaller arms to repel boats and harry infantry men. And down the coast, about a mile away, close by Yeni Shehr village, stood the fourth of the forts, Orkanieh.

They were old, these bastions of brick and mortar and sandbags and stuffed cloth. It appeared simple enough, given the modern weapons of the British Navy, to knock them out in a few hours and then move on. Whether or not a landing would be necessary, remained to be seen.

On 18 February, the officers of the fleet were making ready, and none more certainly than those of *Ark Royal*, the seaplane carrier, whose effectiveness was to be tried out in this operation. The battleship men, by and large, were as suspicious of the airplane as they were of the submarine. And yet they could see how aircraft might some day become stable enough to be used for observation of battles and assist the gunners in their work.

In 1911, a Short biplane had been flown from a trackway of the forecastle of HMS *Africa* when that ship was moored in Sheerness harbour. The experiment had been a shaky success, and the following year the Admiralty had allowed the enthusiasts to make other experiments, flying planes off tracks when ships were moving at speeds up to twelve knots. These efforts were successful enough to occasion more, and in 1913 an eighty-horsepower Caudron seaplane was adapted to a trackway built on the forecastle of the cruiser HMS *Hermes*, and a whole succession of experiments was subsequently carried out. The *Hermes* operations were successful enough, but the admirals did not see how they could adapt cruisers and battleships to airplane usage, because the trackway necessary to put a little plane aloft was so long as to interfere with the guns of the warship.

A number of ideas presented themselves. One was the catapult, which eventually would become standard. Another was the concept of putting a seaplane over the side by crane and letting it take off from there. This had the disadvantage of demanding a stopped ship, which could be fatal in time of war. A third idea occurred to some officers: design a special seaplane carrier which could operate with the fleet and supply the air liaison that nearly everyone now agreed was useful, if it did not interfere with gunnery or ship operation. The problem was to find a ship that could be converted to a carrier without too much trouble or expense. When the Admiralty began looking about, it was not too long before a suitable object presented itself. She was a steamer, just under construction at the Blyth Company yards. The hull was finished, and so some major redesign work had to be done, but not so much as to be impossible. The Admiralty took over this vessel, a hull 353 feet long, fifty feet in the beam, drawing eighteen feet and capable of movement at eleven knots. In the redesign the boilers and engine room were moved aft, and so was the bridge. The vessel was cut back so that the utmost area could be given over to flying space – when the workmen were finished, they had managed to allow a deck 130 feet long. Down below, the hold decks were torn up and made into a single big hangar for aircraft, a space 150 feet long, forty-five feet wide and fifteen feet high, which allowed men to work on the planes down below.

By modern twentieth-century standards, she was a tiny thing, and she carried only ten seaplanes, fragile craft of light wood, metal and precious fabric. They were hoisted to the decks by steam cranes, flown off and then hoisted down again, for testing and repairs.

At the end of 1913 and in the early months of 1914 the ship was built, the planes were made ready and the tests were carried out to assure her fitness for the sea. She was launched in September and so rapid was the completion of her fixtures thereafter that she was commissioned on 9 September and put in service by Commander R. H. Clark-Hall. So, even as war came, the British Navy was getting ready to develop this new weapon to assist the fleet.

In the November shelling of the Dardanelles, Admiral Carden and his staff complained about weather and spotting and all the difficulties they were having in hitting their targets. They were convinced of the need for aircraft to help them. And it just so happened that Winston Churchill was enthusiastic about the air weapon and that *Ark Royal* was at Harwich, preparing for sea, with an impatient Churchill wondering what she could do to further the war effort.

After the stormy War Council meeting of 28 January, orders were soon given that *Ark Royal* was to join the Dardanelles force and was to be ready to put to sea by the end of the month. She had already received preliminary orders about the mission and the sailing. And on Monday, 1 February, just as the bells struck midnight, she slipped away from her harbour position and the enemy watchers who would have loved to know precisely where she was going, and moved out of Sheerness harbour, bound for the coasts of Asia.

Ark Royal's maiden voyage was a rough baptism in the behaviour of the winter seas. She encountered stiff gales and heavy seas in the Channel, and her passage down the coast of France was not an easy one in this wintry weather. The waves of the Bay of Biscay were like great grey mountains, looking to topple down on her, and she bucked and sprayed her way southwards for a week. Then she crossed around Gibraltar and came into the relative calm of the Mediterranean, arriving at Tenedos on 17 February, to prepare for her share of the work.

First Attempts

Back in London, Churchill and his admirals were giving every consideration to the coming operation against the Turks. On 15 February they turned special attention to the problems of reconnaissance and the condition of those installations bombarded in November. They ordered Carden to commence aerial operations, to check out the condition of the forts and find new installations if any existed.

It was a little difficult, even two days later when *Ark Royal* pulled into harbour, to obey the orders from London. But the seas running at Tenedos that day were not bad – very slight indeed by any but aerial standards – and it was agreed that a flight or two might be chanced. Only the natural enthusiasm of the pilots for their work seemed to be able to keep them in the air at all. For, with one exception, the aircraft assigned to the carrier were not adapted to the work. They were: one Short two-seater, with 200-hp Canton Unné engine; two Wight two-seaters, with 200-hp Canton Unné engines; three Sopwith two-seaters, with 100-hp Monosoupape engines and two Sopwith Tabloid single-seaters, with 80 Gnome engines (the last two were land planes with wheels). Of eight operational planes altogether, only one, the Short, was really adaptable for the job of taking off from the sea, flying over the land and landing again without crashing. The other seven planes might have done very well on a protected lake, but it took virtually nothing in the way of current or chop to make them unnavigable on the surface – and so how well they might fly was scarcely an issue. In a flat calm the suction seemed to make it even harder to get these planes off the water.

The pilots and observers had other complaints. None of the aircraft had sufficient power to carry them to an altitude where they could make best observations. Even when they ran at full power, they had a hard time climbing. The two land planes could not be used at all, because Tenedos had no airfield or fair ground or any surface flat enough and long enough to be cleared for take-off and landing. So there they were, on the eve of the operation, with only six usable machines.

Following orders from Admiral Carden, the aviators began to make ready on 17 February for several observation flights. The first plane was put over the side, and the pilot and observer buckled up their helmets and their belts and made ready to take off. But the engine popped, snorted, emitted great clouds of greasy smoke – and then failed entirely. The plane had to be hoisted back aboard the carrier, and a second was put down. The experience was almost precisely the same – not much of an advertisement for the Naval Air Service. The third plane was put over the side in what an old tar would have called a very calm sea, hardly stirring. The pilot revved up the engine, pointed the nose out to sea and began pushing the throttle forward, stick firmly between his legs, making ready to pull back at the crucial moment and break the suction that held the plane down. But no matter how the pilot raced the engine, and no matter how hard he pulled on the joystick, the little plane would not take off. She shuddered in the impact of the slight sea; she wobbled and careened and stayed on the surface. So, abjectly, pilot and observer brought the seaplane back to the *Ark Royal*, and they, too, were lifted in.

Finally, Flight Lieutenant G.R.Bromet and Flight Commander H.A.Williamson decided to try one of the Wights. Perhaps it could get off the sea where the Sopwiths had failed. Most of the day had already been wasted in the previous abortive attempts at flight. The wind had abated a bit, perhaps, but it never was very strong. The grey of the day concealed the lowering sun – they had best be up and doing if they wanted to carry out the Admiralty orders and save Admiral Carden and the whole Air Service embarrassment.

It was 5.30 in the afternoon before they were in the plane and on the water. Lieutenant Bromet taxied, then he took off and all the troubles of the day seemed to melt away from the deck of *Ark Royal* as his shipmates cheered. He climbed and circled and took the little plane up to four thousand feet, then headed for the forts of the outer defences, to search out the damage of November, if it still showed, and to look for new gun installations along the coast, around the forts and up the Straits for three miles.

First the plane had another experimental mission: the Lieutenant took course for Fort Kum Kale, and there they dropped a twenty-pound bomb, which hit one of the walls and made a highly satisfying cloud of smoke and debris. Then it was around and around the fort, at lower levels, as the small cannon, rifles and machine-guns popped away at the plane. The observer sat in his cockpit, craning and drawing on the map, to mirror what he saw below. And he saw plenty – in the days since that first bombardment, the Germans and the Turks had been busy with replacements and new installations. Trenches had been dug around Cape Tekke – snaky yellow and grey lines showing rawly on the maps. Moving down the peninsula, they saw other new lines of fortifications on the Asiatic coast, south and inland of Fort No. 4 at Orkanieh.

Noting these, noting the damage done to the old forts, and presence of troop installations, the pair of airmen came back, circled and were on the water next to the seaplane carrier at 6.45. They had spent an hour and fifteen minutes aloft and were able to make a report that was most satisfactory to the Carden staff. The Wight seaplane also had seven bullet holes.

11 February Fling

So far, everyone involved had done his job successfully. On 18 February the *Ark Royal* was quiet, her officers and air crews subdued and trying to invent ways to make the aircraft work better in future, for the next day she was to open the effort against the forts.

The morning of the 19th saw the sun rising over the mountains of the east. The men of *Ark Royal* were on deck, labouring quietly but purposefully, as were those of the rest of the British fleet. Steam was up in the boilers, and at half-past seven that morning the seaplane carrier weighed anchor and moved as swiftly as she could to the little island of Mavro. She anchored there just after nine o'clock and waited.

Her reconnaissance flight was already in the air as *Ark Royal* steamed away from Tenedos. This time it was the Short, with her two planes and 200-horsepower Canton Unné engine. No one in the fleet knew it yet, but the Short was the best of the planes for the tasks at hand, and this day she would prove herself and bring much honour to the brave young men who flew her. Flight Commander C.F.Kilner was captain of the plane that day, and his aide was Sub-Lieutenant D.W.Park. Their job was to reconnoitre the Strait for twenty miles, from Besika Bay, eight miles south of the entrance to the Straits, to Gaba Tepe, twelve miles north.

Scarcely had *Ark Royal* made her new anchorage than the plane was back, circling and then landing, and the excited officers came aboard to deliver the desired information. They had ascertained the exact position of the barracks and of Fort No. 1, at Helles. They had also learned a very important fact: that the guns of Cape Tekke were so fixed that they could not fire northwards or north-west and would not be able to hit the ships assigned to firing on that region.

And what else had they seen, asked their seniors? It had been a difficult flight – so early in the morning, in this time of year, the mist hung low along the coastal waters of the Strait, and they had difficulty in seeing the installations. The warming sun helped – after some circling about the Cape Tekke area, they could tell that no new batteries had been placed near Yeni Keui or around Cape Tekke. Soon this information was on its way to Admiral Carden's flagship, to be digested by the staff and passed on to those who could profit from it.

To please the French, Admiral Carden made certain that they had a basic role in the action. *Suffren* was instructed to bombard Kum Kale's Fort No. 6, firing over Cape Yeni Shehr at a range of nine to ten thousand yards. This could hardly have been done without a spotting ship or aircraft – and the weather was much too uncertain for the sustained use of the planes, even had there been a hundred of them and had they all been suited for the task. So *Bouvet*, the second French ship, was assigned to spot for the other, and she moved to a point five miles west of Cape Helles. The third French ship, *Gaulois*, was assigned to patrol Besika Bay, to keep small artillery from harrying the naval force as it moved in.

The British ships were given their tasks: *Triumph* was to bombard Cape Helles, with *Inflexible* spotting; *Cornwallis* was to bombard Fort No. 4 at Orkanieh, from a point where she needed no spotters (west of Cape Yeni Shehr); *Albion*, *Amethyst* and seven minesweepers were to clear out a big area south of Gaba Tepe, for *Queen Elizabeth*.

So the bombardment began that morning at such long range that only the forts at Orkanieh and Ertoghrui even tried to fire back. All day long the ships aimed and fired. After two hours the Admiral called on *Ark Royal* for more information, and Flight Lieutenant Bromet and Flight

Commander Williamson went up again, this time in a Wight. The first point of call was to be Orkanieh, at which *Cornwallis* had fired the very first shot of the day, delivered at 9.51. After two hours of firing on this fort, something ought to have been accomplished, and the pilot and observer were to discover just what.

They circled lazily. It was not a difficult task – none of the land was more than three hundred feet high, the mist had risen and the weather was as fine as anyone might expect. They took a look at the installations at Yeni Shehr and then droned on up to the west and inland, to find the fort at Orkanieh, lying spreadeagled in the sun beneath them. From on high they saw the guns in clear detail, standing silent. Not a shot was fired at them or at the ships on the sea, and the airmen took courage and circled lower for a better look. Still, silence.

The observer got on his wireless and tapped out the message. The guns were not hurt yet, but it could be only a matter of time with this accurate spotting technique. He gave map co-ordinates and geographical information about the fort to the gunners of *Cornwallis*. Then he waited, preparing to report to the ship below and behind them as to the placement of the fire of the big guns.

Cornwallis was silent. For an hour Bromet flew back and forth across the fortress, maintaining an altitude above rifle fire for the most part. And the airmen waited.

Aboard *Cornwallis* the guns were silent. Earlier in the morning, after the original shots had been fired, Admiral Carden had ordered – more or less as an afterthought – that the battleships drop anchor and thus stabilize their shooting platforms for the gunners. *Cornwallis* moved to comply and then was dreadfully embarrassed – her capstan broke down and the bow anchors simply could not be dropped until it was repaired.

As the airmen circled and tried to make contact with the ship, they thought at first that something was wrong with the wireless. Then they thought that something must be wrong with the ship. Finally, they moved away and headed out to complete their mission before they ran out of petrol. They were to fly over the various other forts and report on the damage done by the first two hours of bombardment. They found that Orkanieh's guns were intact but vulnerable, as were the guns at Kum Kale and Sedd-el-Bahr.

Back at the carrier, they forwarded the reports. From the planes and other observations, Admiral Carden learned that two of the forts had suffered serious damage and that two others were hit hard. But those forts with the open earthworks – the small new ones – were harder to hit, and it was more difficult to estimate the damage done. Also, because the Turks and their German teachers were intelligent men, they kept the guns quiet, particularly when the airplanes were about, for there was little use in firing at the ships, far out of range, while to bring down an aircraft, yet suffer destruction by the vengeful guns in retaliation, would have been suicidal.

So the guns continued to fire. *Vengeance* replaced *Cornwallis* in the line and started shooting at Orkanieh fort. By two o'clock the thundering from the ships had been heard for nearly five hours, and Admiral Carden was so satisfied with the damage inflicted that he felt it time to institute the second half of the day's plan. He gave the signal for six of his ships to advance towards the coast and begin close bombardment of the forts. The continued silence from the land had led the Admiral to believe that the Turkish installations were nearly demolished.

The minesweepers went ahead, doing their work, and the grey warships followed.

Unfortunately, *Queen Elizabeth*, the pride of the fleet, had still not arrived on station, although the big ship *Agamemnon* came into position during the afternoon and was able to participate in the battle. Carden was surprised – as were the commanders of the ships – when the British and French vessels came inshore, close enough for the guns to be effective. For the Turks had not lost heart – nor were their installations so badly damaged as the optimistic reports of the gun-spotters had told Admiral Carden. The forts started up a brisk return fire as the ships came in. The forts on the European side, which had borne the brunt of fire in the morning, and accurate fire at that, seemed to be silenced. But those on the mainland, or Asiatic side, were not silent at all. Quite to the contrary, they began to give a good account of themselves.

The gunners of *Triumph* spotted several bodies of troops moving on the shore and concentrated fire on them for a time. *Ark Royal* sent up another plane to spot for *Vengeance*, but they lost contact, and the effort failed.

Meanwhile, in the forts, the day's activity had brought colour and cheer to the faces of the Turks and Germans. For too long they had stood waiting, while the cursed enemy offshore made his plans to attack. Action was far preferable. And from the Turkish standpoint the action was proceeding very satisfactorily. By mid-afternoon, the British thought they had silenced the forts, and Admiral Carden so wrote. But not long after four o'clock, *Suffren* came in close enough to Orkanieh to see that *all* the guns were intact, and she made ready to give them a going over. Then the language problem intervened, a confirmatory message from Admiral Carden was misread and *Suffren* hauled off, as the Turks cheered.

In one fort German Obermaat Erwin Bossert led the cheering, for as the British ships came in close that afternoon he had directed the firing of his big gun, and he swore that of eighteen shots fired at the British, fourteen struck British ships. Alas, it was an illusion. The fact was that neither side was damaged – the British vessels not at all. The Turks at the High Command level were under no such illusions; Admiral von Usedom's defenders made no claims to having hurt the enemy. And in the official despatch Admiral Carden was careful to note that while various reports of hits and damage were made by the ships and gunners concerned, the effect of the bombardment on the earthworks seemed to be slight. There was a good number of hits on Forts 1 and 6, and earth and stones went flying in a most satisfactory way. Twelve-inch shells striking thus must do some damage – and yet, when the ships closed in on the forts, the fire was so intense in return that Rear-Admiral Keyes believed for a time, from his post aboard *Inflexible*, that the big ship *Vengeance* had actually been hit. The forts at Orkanieh and Helles were doing good work.

Late in the afternoon two more seaplanes took off to try to spot for the fleet on the Helles fort, which was regarded as the single most important one. But the planes both had trouble with their wireless. The aerial on one plane jammed and would not release – so it had to give up. The wireless set on the second plane short-circuited, much to the disgust of the pilot and his observer – and so all that work and opportunity was lost.

At the end of the day, the airplanes were still flying, until dusk brought them down. The pilots reported that the guns of No. 1 Fort were intact, still standing about thirty yards from the edge of the cliff that protected them. At five o'clock, when they flew over Sedd-el-Bahr and Kum Kale, the pall of smoke from incoming shells and fire from the forts was so great that the pilots could see nothing in detail.

And so the day ended. At 5.30 the order to withdraw was signalled, and at 7.30 that night *Ark Royal* hoisted in her last seaplane and her screws began turning, to carry her back to the safe anchorage at Tenedos.

That night in the wardrooms of the fleet, the events of the day were discussed. Aboard the *Ark Royal* all the talk was about the planes and their performance, and the difficulties of spotting for bombardment. It was a new game, and there was much to be learned, as the pilots and observers had realized already. There was a good deal of disappointment in the fleet about the failure of the planes in which so many had put so much faith. But the difficulties had to be solved.

First of all, a reasonable system of ship-to-air visual communications must be developed. Had the men of the morning known of the difficulties of *Cornwallis* with her anchor, they might have been off on more important business, or they might have got into contact with *Vengeance* later and done a good job of spotting for her. But until this time, so little attention had been paid by the naval authorities to air operations that no adequate spotter system existed.

Indeed, on this day, while the ships did their shooting, the War Council was again meeting in London and coming to certain conclusions, not all of them very worthy. Winston Churchill was still convinced that the fall of the forts of Liège and Namur had shown that permanent fortifications could be knocked out by long-range guns. That fact had not yet been proved one way or the other, because *Queen Elizabeth*, with her fifteen-inch guns, had missed the first day's action. But aboard the vessels of Carden's little fleet there was a considerable degree of scepticism, for many a gunner had noted what effect those twelve-inch shells did *not* have.

The War Council members were impressed with the use of aircraft – which was more prescient of them at that moment than due to any real results obtained in the Dardanelles action. And they were impressed by the development of the submarine, hoping that the exploits of *B-11* could be improved upon in the next few months.

The Council was now of two minds. One set of actions was to have the utmost effect on the future of the Dardanelles operation. For in recent days, while all had gone right ahead with their work on the naval bombardment, Admiral Fisher and other professionals had been much heartened with the information that soon the operation would be a joint command, with a large landing force and army behind it, to support the naval bombardment and force the waterway to the Sea of Marmara.

On this day, 19 February, much seemed to have changed, for Lord Kitchener came to the meeting and astounded the assembled naval people there by announcing that the 29th Division would not be made available for the Dardanelles. To this bad news he added a little good: the Australian and New Zealand divisions that had recently come to train in Egypt would be made available for the operation instead. Anyone who knew his command tables would know that this was not a fair exchange. The 29th was a trained division, but the Australian and New Zealand troops were green, and it was questionable if they had yet had the time to absorb the steel that would make fighting men of them and keep them alive in desperate circumstances. Winston Churchill erupted with a loud complaint, and he was backed by his regular naval subordinates. But there was no changing Kitchener's mind.

All this while, Churchill's plan for striking the enemy in the south had been developing in his own mind, and he now thought in terms of having fifty thousand men to hit in conjunction with the naval forcing of the Straits.

In his artful manner, Churchill brought forth the argument that the best way of relieving the increasingly bad situation of the Russians was to come up from the south. And when he saw that Lord Kitchener was unmovable, Churchill presented one new argument that he had not previously enunciated. Perhaps, on sober consideration and after discussions with Fisher and others, Churchill had learned some of the detail of naval warfare that he had not known before. In any event, he told an astonished Council that it would be impossible for the fleet alone to keep the Dardanelles open for merchant shipping, once the Sea of Marmara was reached, even once the *Goeben* and *Breslau* were destroyed.

Then why? Why this action that had commenced a few hours earlier and was still committed to the forcing of the sea lane? The vital question went unasked that day. Perhaps the War Council members had too many different problems on their minds to see what had changed. Perhaps the detail of their arguments confused and diverted them – for Kitchener at this meeting did agree to send a small force from Egypt to help the fleet immediately which meant more occupying troops if they were needed. Good as his word, he ordered Lieutenant General John Maxwell to make ready thirty thousand men for movement to the Dardanelles area in a few days. Maxwell was to be in touch with Admiral Carden, to ascertain just what Carden needed for his operation and to try to give it to him. So it was left at that, and the forces of fate ground on inexorably.

12   The Optimists

In London, Winston Churchill called 20 February 'day of recoil'. He was still stunned by the turn of events of the previous day at the War Council. Later he was to write that he felt as though Kitchener had not only refused him the trained 29th Division of regulars but that somehow Kitchener had cooled dreadfully on the Dardanelles operation. He had a letter from Kitchener, a rather grumbling letter, talking ostensibly of the hope of the General that they would not have to put up with any Frenchmen in the Dardanelles operation. But the grumbling obviously went deeper than that, and the shrewd Churchill sensed that something was going definitely astray, although he could not at that moment put his finger on it.

Churchill had really come around in many ways to Fisher's position – the First Lord of the Admiralty was gathering transports at Alexandria for forty thousand men. Now he felt subverted, and even more so when Kitchener sent his personal aide to see Fisher. Colonel Fitzgerald, the aide, came into the First Sea Lord's room and announced that it was definite that the 29th Division would not embark for the Dardanelles and that thus all the prepared transport would not be needed. Fisher assumed, as he had every right to do, that this agreement had been made between Churchill and Kitchener. After all, no gentleman of the service would either lie or misinform another. And so Fisher cancelled the orders for the gathering of the sea forces at Alexandria; the word went out to the director of Naval Transport, and the ships began to disperse, without the slightest knowledge of Winston Churchill.

It was a sign of the will of men to believe what they want to believe that, in spite of Carden's laconic and truthful report of the first day's bombardment activities, Churchill, when he read the words, was able to retain his optimism. There was, of course, the unknown factor: *Queen Elizabeth* had not participated, and she was the central figure in the whole affair. At least no ships had been touched, and much had been learned. Perhaps the Churchillian optimism was justified. On the morning of 20 February, the planes of *Ark Royal* were ready, but the weather was not. The day dawned misty with a low overcast sky which precluded any observation or any effective flying for that matter. So the men of the carrier worried about their communications defects and set about doing what they could to remedy them. These were days of learning, these early moments of the war's adventure. The signalmen and the aviators took it upon themselves at this point to begin devising radio-wireless sets suitable for the aircraft. They also pointed out to their superiors the need for a visual signalling system between aircraft and ships, and the need for a code in which to signal. But as for operations, the aircraft were confined to the hangar and the deck of *Ark Royal*, and would be for five long days as the seas tossed and the grey skies glowered above them.

The fleet was anchored off Tenedos that morning, the Admiral hoping to join the battle again and disappointed that the weather impeded operations. But there was much to be done. Carden conferred with his second-in-command, Admiral de Robeck, and the French commander, Admiral Guepratte, and he sent the ships to try their hand again, even in the execrable conditions of the day. The ships did send out fingers of barrage, at close range for a time, and they came back to report that the Orkanieh battery was wrecked. At least it was silent. That was only mildly satisfactory news to the Admiral. Rather less satisfactory was the word that the Turks were moving a large number of men about the land area of the Asian side of the Dardanelles and that the torpedo boats were giving signs that they were getting ready to go into action. In the afternoon the big Allied ships were called back. Carden had no desire to be the recipient of a torpedo boat attack that evening and, knowing that the Germans were in charge of Turkish defences, he played cautiously.

He was quite right. The fact was that the Germans and Turks had split the Turkish defences on a line drawn from east to west from the Bosporus to the Dardanelles. The First Turkish Army would operate on the north side of this line, and the Second Turkish Army on the south.

It was ironic – for the Turkish dispositions left the Dardanelles very lightly defended and the Gallipoli peninsula at that moment almost totally undefended. It was as if the Germans had guessed that the British were not sending an army to join the naval attackers after all. And even as the Turks and Germans moved, the War Council in London hesitated and argued about matters that had apparently been agreed a few days earlier.

A strong south-west gale blew up on 21 February, and, as such storms do, it reminded Carden and his staff that they faced as much or more danger from the sea as they ever would from the guns of the Germans and the Turks. In these conditions the sea must be minded, and the plans of men to war against each other must be put aside. The visibility was dreadful. There was no possibility of firing on the forts with any chance of hitting anything, even were a commander fool enough to risk his vessels. So they moved to the lee of Tenedos and huddled there, bobbing in the wind and splashed by the might of nature, until evening began to make the grey greyer, and the coming of black streaks in the mist showed the onset of night. Then, in obedience to the commander's instructions, the whole fleet moved out to a cold and tossing night on the open sea, safe only from the possibility of submarine or torpedo boat attacks, endangered more by nature once again.

Next day the weather persisted bad, so Admiral Carden had to suspend operations again. The ships fought the weather and waited, and the officers listened to the wireless to gain what little information they might from neutral stations and from Reuter dispatches sent out from Egypt. They listened to Constantinople but heard only wild claims of Turkish victories.

The 22nd was overcast, and wind was blowing and, as the light strengthened, so did the storm, making it impossible to fly airplanes or even spot guns from more than a few hundred yards. And so operations were suspended again, and the fleet coaled, for lack of other useful occupation. The officers and men kept up their spirits with hot tea and infusions of promises as to the damage they were going to do the Turks on the morrow. The evening seemed better, almost as though nature would promise a day of sun and battle, and the night was fairly calm in the area of Tenedos. But the morning of the 23rd smashed in on the shoulders of another storm. The fleet was having lessons in seamanship; unlashed gear washed overboard, and several officers lost their binoculars to the depths because they were not securely fastened.

In Constantinople, the Germans believed the Turkish reports of the damage done by the guns against the fleet and put out a wireless report to the world to the effect that the British flagship was so badly damaged in the first day's fighting that the devils had not had the nerve to come back since. How *that* annoyed Admiral Carden!

Each day, in spite of the storm, the effects of Winston Churchill's ideas and the planning of his naval staff became more apparent. On 24 February, in spite of dreadful weather, HMS *Dartmouth* arrived at Tenedos with Admiral Rosslyn Wemyss aboard, and the Admiral paid his call on Carden. Wemyss had been placed in charge of the base that had been rented from the Greeks. Having checked in, he headed for Lemnos and the arduous task of preparing for the reception of troops. Meanwhile, each night the fleet left Tenedos and its shelter and headed out to sea to avoid mishap with the Turkish defenders. And each morning dawned in hope that faded as the day turned greyer and stormier than the previous one. It was such dreadful weather that the trans-shipment of supplies and baggage was suspended, so that new officers arriving for duty had to beg or borrow toothbrushes and shaving tackle.

On the night of 24 February, *Majestic* arrived, to add her big guns to the force. There were plenty of ships now to do the job. All Carden was waiting for was a bit of sunshine so he could move in and finish those forts.

Back in London the War Council was muddling. There can be no other description for what was happening, and in the light of history it was ridiculous. The Turks and Germans had made the decision to leave the coast of Gallipoli and the Asiatic coast at the mouth of the Dardanelles undefended by troops. If the Allies could make a landing in the next few weeks, they would find the going easy all the way to Constantinople. But not only had the War Office decided not to send the 29th Division of regulars, the sea train had been disorganized.

On 24 February, as the winds blew at Tenedos, and the ships struggled in the high seas, the War Council met again. And once again the men who were entrusted with running the British war changed their collective mind.

The news from Carden was indecisive. He had begun the bombardment but had not knocked out all the forts, that much was sure. Yet the naval men in the Council chose to be optimistic on the basis of the dispatches, and the military and civilians could not but follow suit. Kitchener had now decided that he was going to have to use the New Zealand and Australian troops to back up the fleet at the Dardanelles. He told General Maxwell, the commander in Egypt, to make ready to send the thirty thousand men under Lieutenant General Sir W.R.Birdwood. But the transports in Egypt having been dispersed, it was going to take until 9 March to embark the men from Egypt, and that was a big difference from the matter of days it would have been otherwise. The solution advocated by Kitchener was for Maxwell to begin again assembling ships, and piecemeal to send troops to Lemnos, for no one knew when the bombarding force would have taken its first objectives and how many troops would be needed to go ashore and hold them. It seemed an odd way to fight a war.

On 23 February, as the winds howled off the Turkish coast, General Maxwell found that he had transports for a brigade, but he did not have all the supplies from England for the troops that would be dispatched. Someone seemed to be forgetting that provisioning and maintenance of an army was an immensely complicated task. For example, what would they do for horses? The number of horses to be found on Lemnos was going to be extremely limited. And on looking about, Maxwell discovered that only four horseboats were at Alexandria and none at all in Malta – the assembled multitude having been shipped back to England to alleviate a shortage of Channel craft there. General Maxwell sent Admiral Carden a message: how many ships and what supplies and what men did he need? Carden blenched. This was not his purview, he insisted. He was the servant of London, which had devised the plan.

Once again, the principle of limited responsibility was serving the British war effort very badly. Carden, when he had been asked by Churchill to devise a plan for an assault on the Dardanelles, had approached the matter as a draftsman, not as a commander. Here on the scene he took the position that the plan was London's and that he was a slave to it. He sent a message to Maxwell: 'I have been directed to make preparations for landing a force of ten thousand men if such a step is found necessary; at present my instructions go no further. If such a force is sent, I would propose landing it at Sedd-el-Bahr with the object of occupying the Gallipoli peninsula as far east as the Soghanii Dere-Chaan-vova.'

So the confusion grew worse. In London Lord Kitchener thought that the Navy knew what they were about. In Egypt General Maxwell now knew better, but Winston Churchill did not. Equally strange at this moment, and adding to the confusion, was the sad state of the military intelligence available to the War Council – possibly because the War Council had not yet consulted once with the British General Staff about this whole matter. The Councillors suddenly learned that Gallipoli was 'occupied' by forty thousand Turkish troops. (Actually there were no more than a handful of soldiers on the whole peninsula.) Kitchener was so upset at this information, and at the apparent plan to occupy the peninsula with ten thousand troops, that he ordered Birdwood to rush to the Dardanelles, find Admiral Carden and discover just what was happening. Would troops be needed, or would they not?

On 24 February Kitchener was in touch with General Maxwell too, more or less thinking out loud, musing over the possibility: would ten thousand troops assault forty thousand troops, or were no troops at all needed? That same day, Winston Churchill had the Admiralty send an equally confusing message to Admiral Carden, indicating that no one in London seemed to know precisely what was happening or what was to be done.

And there was a reason. The War Councillors had quite forgotten, in their moving of men and ships around the chessboard, that every action of theirs had several reactions, not the least of which was world opinion. When the word came out, through Reuters and the German and Turkish news dispatches, that the British 'fleet' was attacking the forts of the Dardanelles, amateur strategists the world over grew excited with the prospects of this change in the fortunes of the war. What had been planned as a show of force, a diversion which could be abandoned if it did not go well, suddenly became something quite different, with the entire prestige of Britain and her naval might thrown into the balance.

Lloyd George, who attended War Council meetings sporadically and had little part in the previous weeks' plans, came to the meeting on 24 February to raise a whole new series of objections. He did not believe that the Dardanelles operation had been carried through – as was now the general opinion. He wanted to do what others had suggested earlier: if the Dardanelles operation failed, then the fleet and army should land somewhere else, perhaps at Alexandretta, and make believe that the whole had been an immense feint from the beginning.

But Winston Churchill announced that the country was absolutely committed to the Dardanelles attack. Lord Kitchener, the military man, agreed with him. Sir Edward Grey, the Foreign Minister, agreed. The Prime Minister agreed.

And that is how the policy was made.

13   Bombardment Renewed

On 25 February, the sun came out, and the rippling grey of sea and sky was replaced by the blue and green of decent weather. It was not an airman's dream, unluckily: the water was so choppy from the storm and the aftermath winds that the seaplanes could not take off no matter how they tried that morning. But Admiral Carden and his forces were eager to be at work, and the weather was good enough to let them proceed. Time now seemed even more vital to the programme than earlier. General Birdwood was on his way – he had sailed from Egypt with a brigade, and a French division was promised by 1 March.

From London, the planner, Sir Henry Jackson, was assuring Admiral Carden that he could make haste slowly; he did not need to occupy the southern end of the peninsula just then. He should wait for Birdwood's arrival and then make plans for occupation.

How the ball bounced is evident here. Carden was in charge; he was not in charge; Birdwood was to be in charge; or London was in charge. The fact was that no one at this moment was in charge, and it showed all too clearly. But the bombardment, having been ordered and having drawn the enthusiasm of these thousands of men and these big warships, was proceeding on its own account.

Queen Elizabeth was on hand, and she and *Agamemnon* began booming forth their fire before 10.30 in the morning, the *Queen* taking on Fort No. 3, *Agamemnon* supporting her. The fifteen-inch guns sent out their hail of fire, smoke and explosives time after time. Shortly after the engagement began, the German officers in Fort No. 1 showed their excellence. *Agamemnon* was firing when the Turks seemed to get the range and before her commander knew it, *Agamemnon* had been straddled, hit once, and had to move in a hurry.

Irresistible took Fort No. 4, and just before eleven o'clock that morning a great cheer rose up, because she had made several direct hits, the last of which silenced the fort for the day.

At noon came another cheer. Through the glasses the men in the fleet were watching the destructive power of *Queen Elizabeth*'s fifteen-inch guns on the stone and earth of Fort No. 1. A shell, a tremendous explosion, and one gun in Fort No. 1 was dismounted. Fifteen minutes later *Irresistible* knocked out a gun in Fort No. 4.

Given this advantage, the *Vengeance* and *Cornwallis* began to run past the forts, edging in closer on each pass, firing at Forts 1 and 4. The forts did not return the fire, and when the ships had finished the last run, at 1.22, from the inshore observations the intelligence officers reported that Fort No. 1 was deserted and all its guns dismounted; Fort No. 4 was also deserted although her guns were still in position. Only Fort No. 3 was still firing, on *Vengeance*.

The fleet regrouped, and in the afternoon the French took the lead. *Suffren* went in for a run, followed at three thousand yards by *Charlemagne*, and they fired at three of the forts that might possibly still be active. Only one of them replied with any fire at all. *Triumph*, *Albion* and *Vengeance* took position outside the minefield and began firing at suspected smaller gun positions, to soften them up for the minesweepers. It would do no good to send sweepers in to brave the minefields only to have them demolished by accurate fire from guns on the shore.

At three o'clock *Albion* and *Triumph* moved in, about a mile from the south and north shores, to destroy those guns. From three of the forts came single shots – and then silence. The British warships fired on anything that moved, slowly, regularly, patiently, for a solid hour. By that time nothing was moving, and when the trawlers came up, they were unmolested. The cruisers, battleships and half a dozen destroyers swept back and forth watchfully, but the only noise was that of the ships' propellers and the shouts of fighting men as they searched the coastal area for unknown minefields. No mines were found – they had not expected them, for intelligence reports had placed the minefields much closer in, and in the dreadful weather of the past few days the Turks would not have been able to lay a field, even had they possessed the mines at that time.

At the end of the day the Turkish forts were all silent. The only enemy action came from the hills, where late in the afternoon concealed howitzers began a peppering action that was most erratic if a bit unnerving. The only four long-range Turkish guns seemed to have been destroyed. As for the howitzers, they might have been knocked out by fire directed from the seaplanes, but the weather never did ease enough that day to enable the aircraft to take off from the choppy water.

That night the airwaves were busy. The Turks claimed a tremendous victory. *Agamemnon*, they said, had been badly hurt (she had been hurt but not badly); *Gaulois* had also been hit by six-inch shells fired by an accurate gunner inshore. The Turks made much of this – and nothing of the fact that the forts were silenced.

The first objective of the Dardanelles operation had proved successful, with only a handful of casualties, and without the loss of a single vessel.

By now, the whole Dardanelles picture had changed, and nothing indicates that change more fully than an interview between Lord Kitchener and Colonel Valantin of the French liaison office in London. The Colonel came to see the War Minister in order to clarify the British position on the Dardanelles and send that information to the War Minister in Paris.

The 'expedition' was the way Kitchener now referred to the Dardanelles; it was no longer an 'operation'. But of course times had changed. In the original planning there was no talk about the Bulgarians being in the war on the side of the Germans. Now there was. Originally there had been a psychological value to be exerted against the Bulgars, the Rumanians and the Austrians, and to push the Greeks and the Italians. All these positions had become different in the march of war politics.

On the night of 25 February Admiral Carden and his staff were up late, planning. Commodore Keyes, the Chief of Staff to Carden, took a destroyer over to *Vengeance* from *Inflexible*. There he made arrangements with Admiral de Robeck for the next day's schedule.

The sweepers worked again that night. In the morning they came under fire from the concealed guns in the hills, and Admiral Carden was eager to have the 'flies', as the seaplanes were known, up to buzz about and spot those annoying enemy field-guns. The seaplanes were still having their troubles: choppy water and their own lack of power for this work.

Carden could not wait. He sent several ships in to shell the forts again from inside the Straits. *Majestic* was hit once, but that was all. Death and destruction to a few, that was the way of war, with the rest of the officers and ratings untouched by the hand of the enemy. *Vengeance* replied, shelling Achilles' Tomb, where the Turks had positioned men and a gun. By afternoon Admiral Carden was half beside himself with worry. He was sick and nervous, and the way things were going did not at all appeal to his sense of reasonable operation. Nor, he knew, would Churchill accept anything less than total success.

All day long, Chief of Staff Keyes had been moving about the fleet, gathering information and carrying it to his commander. Keyes had gone inside to see the sweepers and had been fired upon by the concealed guns. At 10.30 he hoped to see the seaplanes in the air, but no such luck. So he went to Tenedos, to the flagship, and talked to Carden; they decided that the Marines would be sent in soon to cover demolition parties that would blow up the remaining guns and munitions of the forts. Carden counselled delay – he wanted those seaplanes up and about before he committed even a thousand marines to a land operation.

Keyes went away unsatisfied. There *was* a problem. Like so many nagging, deadly mosquitoes, the small guns of the Turks and Germans continued a harassing fire on the ships and boats which dared move in towards the Turkish shores.

The day wore on. The seaplanes still did not fly, and when they did manage to get into the air, Pilot Kilner and Observer Park returned to report that three guns along the southeast front of the fort at Sedd-el-Bahr, three more at Kum Kale and one gun at Helles, were operating again.

It was too late then to disembark the thousand marines from the *Braemar Castle* which was at Tenedos, but it was not too late for the ships to send in their own demolition parties – and that was the course of action to be followed. Brave men were only waiting for a chance like this. Keyes fully supported the idea, for in *Grasshopper* he was moving about the Dardanelles, seeking spots for the ships to locate and try to wipe out the guns that were annoying them. The Germans were smart, no doubt about it; they were making the absolute best use of the limited supply of weapons at hand. They had given up trying to man the forts that came under the big gun fire, but they had not yielded their position.

At 2.30 in the afternoon the signal sounded, and *Vengeance* and *Irresistible* landed their demolition parties in the small boats, the sailors pulling manfully for the shore, even under fire. Five warships stood offshore to protect the troops with their guns; the men of *Vengeance* headed for Kum Kale, those of *Irresistible* for Sedd-el-Bahr.

Majestic was still firing on the forts, and as Keyes came by her in a whaleboat, he saw her hit several times by six-inch shells, though suffering no serious damage from the forts on which she trained her guns. Keyes could also see a stream of Turks and Germans heading inland, to the hills, away from the deadly rain of fire.

Just then, a six-inch high-explosive shell burst alongside the whaler and made twenty-four holes in her. Then came another, just overshooting, carrying away the wireless telegraphy aerial. Commodore Keyes watched as the concealed guns began dropping shells among the minesweepers. These ships were nothing more than civilian fishing boats, and they could not stand much punishment, so the Commodore realized that he must take swift action to assure their safety. He found Admiral de Robeck and suggested that the sweepers be ordered out of the danger zone until after dark, when they might come in and check once more for signs of enemy action.

Keyes boarded *Vengeance*, so that he might watch the demolition party working on the Asian shore to cut down the guns of those forts. 'It was a very pretty little fight,' he said. He stood on the bridge and through his glasses saw the tars move into the fort and then out again, high up a hill to the edge of a graveyard where the defenders had moved to take cover.

Communications could not have been better. The British Navy signalmen wigged and wagged their flags, and on the ship their fellows understood. Soon *Vengeance* was delivering fire to the assigned spot, the Turkish graveyard. After five minutes the barrage was lifted, and the shore party moved in on the territory. The enemy had evacuated, leaving helmets, bits of uniform and weapons behind. It was a fine haul: the marines and bluejackets took a new battery that had been installed so recently that the earth was still fresh, several light guns and pompoms that would have harried the sweepers when they came in. Keyes was certain that this battery was one of those concealed so well, which had been doing damage to the British and French forces during the afternoon. It was not done without cost. A sergeant of marines was killed, and three marines were badly wounded in the action. They would not underestimate the Turks next time.

Meanwhile, on the European shore the fight was going even harder. The *Irresistible* had sent her party ashore there, but the resistance was stiff. Soon two men were wounded, and for a time it seemed that the party would be pinned down. Then, when the demolition men laid their charges, they went off too soon; the party was close by, and two more men were injured by falling masonry and debris. Those magazines had contained a lot of powder.

As the day ended, the troops were withdrawn and reported back to their commanders. To Carden on his flagship came the bits and pieces that soon rounded out the picture. The guns in Forts 3, 4 and 6 were destroyed, as were two new guns found in Achilles' Tomb.

The marines landed next day, fought a hard fight at Fort No. 1, never did succeed in dislodging the enemy and were finally called back. The weather turned foul again. The seaplanes could not fly, the seas stormed and raged, and the ships could not find a patch of visibility that would encourage them to action. So the invaders stood offshore once more and waited, while Admiral Carden examined the results of his first prolonged bombardment.

It was not as good a job as he had expected. He estimated that seventy per cent of the guns had been intact on their mountings at the end of the bombardment. Many of their magazines had been destroyed. Their electrical communications were shot up. He suggested that the Turks and Germans would have to have several days of uninterrupted work to put the guns into firing condition again. But the belief of Winston Churchill and others in London that big guns could easily knock out fortress defences had been carried too far – so much was certain. In other words, the basic premise of the Dardanelles naval operation had been found wanting before the first day of March, when casualties were only a handful, and when the major commitment of the British to the operation was a moral one.

However, by the end of February the march of events had locked the British into the Dardanelles operation. In St Petersburg the streets echoed with talk of the marvellous British offensive that would soon open the Black Sea to aid from abroad. Even in Constantinople the gloom of the Turks reflected a general belief that the Allies would storm the Straits successfully. Turkish headquarters was preparing for the evacuation of the Sultan and his palace servants, guards and harem. The whole Court would be moved far inland on the Asian side, out of danger.

This fatalism of the Turks caused them to mount their defences in a way that General von Sanders criticized at every opportunity. They would be destroyed, he warned, unless they protected the Dardanelles and Gallipoli. As February ended, the Turks heard him, for they admitted in Constantinople that the entrance forts had now been wiped out and that the British had penetrated well beyond the mouth of the Dardanelles. There was now no question of turning back.

14   The Ides of March

Constantinople was in panic. The news of the penetration
of the Strait soon reached the city. When, after a few days of
extremely rough weather, the British ships moved again
Director Djambolat of the department of public safety began
informing neutral ambassadors that it was time to leave the
capital. Turkish women and children were already being
evacuated, he said, and soon only the soldiers would remain
to face Allah-knew-not-what.

American Ambassador Henry Morgenthau soon discovered
that the banks had sent their gold into Asia to escape capture;
the government archives had been sent to Eskisehir; half the
embassies of Constantinople were already evacuated, and
their secret papers burned or moved out. The Turks were
virtually ready to give up the Dardanelles and concentrate
their forces around Adrianople.

In London, the War Council was like a nest of angrily
buzzing bees. Never before during the war had these men
been pitted against one another as they were now. Winston
Churchill argued incessantly in the time allowed for the
retention of one division of regular troops to lead the invasion
of Gallipoli and investment of the Asian shore, but Lord
Kitchener was obdurate, and even the Prime Minister's
personal plea for the 29th Division left the War Minister
unmoved. At one meeting Churchill so far forgot protocol as
to declare that he would take no further personal responsibility for what happened in the fighting to come if he did
not get that division. It was an impossible statement – the
only way the First Lord of the Admiralty could avoid further

responsibility was to resign, but it at least showed the others how strongly Churchill now felt that the Dardanelles operation must be extended and moved swiftly to achieve its aims.

After the meeting on 26 February, with the reports from Carden generally favourable, Churchill said that he had a feeling of unease. He waited after the meeting and did something quite unusual: he made a personal plea to the Prime Minister to use his authority to insist on the despatch of the 29th Division to the east. But the Prime Minister knew very well that to do so would be to risk the resignation of Lord Kitchener, and who could take that general's place in the scheme of British policy? So Asquith temporized.

'I felt at that moment in an intense way a foreboding of disaster,' said Churchill. 'I knew it was a turning point in the struggle.' Churchill's hopes now – only half-hopes at best – were that Kitchener would change his mind. The whole world, it seemed, was preparing for a major military move at the Dardanelles in the next few days. General Sir William Birdwood had arrived off Tenedos and was conferring with Admiral Carden. And the ships were coming in – the latest of them *Swiftsure* – until now there were fourteen British battleships on hand, plus four French battleships and many light cruisers, destroyers, submarines and the seaplane carrier.

A Dr Lederer, the war correspondent of the *Berliner Tageblatt*, went to the front and returned to report that the German and Turkish officers along the Dardanelles were completely dispirited. 'They were wearing their shrouds', prepared to die in defence of hopeless positions. The Greeks, the Russians, the Bulgars and the Germans were getting as worked up as was Churchill about the implication of what was happening.

At the Admiralty Churchill marshalled figures and facts and bombarded Lord Kitchener with arguments as to the need for the use of trained troops to follow up the advantage they had found at the Dardanelles.

*   *   *

The Russian offensive in the east was paralysed that winter, and the spectre of the French was that the Germans might be able to transfer as many as a million men to the western front. That is why the French objected so strenuously to any transfer of regular British troops to a southern operation. This change had come about in the period since the Dardanelles plan was launched. The Western Front had stabilized, and it was apparent that no one was going to launch a successful offensive right away. This had also changed drastically, at least twice, since the Dardanelles operation began.

Sensing stalemate at the moment, Churchill believed that the only chance of the Allies to seize the initiative was in the 'soft underbelly'. Events of the last few weeks had pushed him back to that old position – subconsciously he must never have left it and must from the first have conceived of the 'limited' naval operation as a foot in the door to await the march of events. That is not to say that Winston Churchill was dishonest in any way, that he had misled others or himself, but it is to say that he proved the creature of his imagination one more time.

Now, knowing what he did of events and progress, he spun a dream: if Lord Kitchener would give him what he wanted, he could take the Allies into Constantinople by the end of March and capture or destroy all Turkish forces in Europe except at Adrianople. The blow would decide the fate of the whole Balkan region, and it would knock out Turkey as a military factor. In this estimate, Churchill had one unwilling supporter who never spoke a word: General Liman von Sanders' appreciation of the situation was almost precisely the same as that of the British First Lord of the Admiralty at that moment.

Churchill wrote to Kitchener, and from the air he found new figures – he could put 115,000 men in the Turkish theatre by 21 March *if Lord Kitchener would move*. (That included twenty thousand French troops and eight thousand

135

Russian troops whose availability was again only in Churchill's dreams.) Together with the glorious navy, they would attack and force the Dardanelles and the Gallipoli peninsula. From that point it was on to Constantinople and mopping up the remnants of the Turks in Europe; the troops could then proceed, probably through Bulgaria (which would reverse its leanings and come into the war on the Allied side) and march on to help the Serbs. Or if the Bulgars stayed neutral, and the Greeks came in, the troops could then march on through Salonika to help the Serbs.

It was complicated; so was Churchill's thinking. The war had many fronts. But because of disagreement and confusion in London, valuable time was being lost. It could mean the difference between success and failure, he knew, and he began to say as much.

On 1 March, the ships took advantage of better weather in the Dardanelles, as if to bear out Churchill's contention that they could clear the passageway's forts of mines and opposition from the shore before the end of the month. Six of the British battleships operated inside the mouth of the Straits. At noon the German and Turkish gunners opened up with field batteries and howitzers, portable guns that were in the declivities and behind the mountains and were hard to find. The Turks had at least twenty howitzers on the Asian side and a dozen on the European side, plus many eight- and six-inch mortars that had been brought in during the last few weeks. So stiff was the fire these field pieces put up that some officers aboard the battleships began to see that unless the guns could be silenced, the traverse of the passage might not be nearly so simple as London had conceived in the beginning. Those guns were much too movable, and they fired and stopped and fired again, so that it was hard to tell when they were 'silenced'.

At noon the guns began to fire on the ships, and half an hour later they ceased. The British had poured a lot of shell into the apparent positions, but they were not under the illusion that all opposition had ended. The Admiral cancelled a new run into shore at one o'clock in fear that the European side's guns might create a good deal of damage. One seaplane was up that day and reported entrenchments and field-gun positions along the whole coast of the Strait.

None the less, the operation must continue; battleships of His Majesty's fleet must not be intimidated by small field-guns of Turkish artillery. So the run in commenced again, early in the afternoon. The ships proceeded towards Dardanos inside the Strait. The Turkish guns on the European side began crackling away; the ships put out strong fire; and the Turks, when the shells began hitting around their positions, had the sensible caution to stop fire in self-protection.

The Turks had not done badly. They had hit five of the six British battleships, some of them repeatedly. They had inflicted casualties – although not heavy ones, because the guns were not large enough to do so. But they were stinging, those Turkish gnats, and forcing the British attackers to do some hard thinking about their prospects and their plans.

Late afternoon saw more landing parties – marines rowed ashore and destroyed the battery at one fort. During the night trawlers and destroyers came in near the shore, and the night was brightened by the spitting of the Turkish small arms and small gun fire as the ships came by.

On 2 March, another cold wintry day, it was noon before the ships could get into motion in the bad weather. Again an exercise in shooting skills developed, and the gun crews of Fort No. 8 were driven out of their hiding places by a series of well placed shells from *Canopus*, *Swiftsure* and *Cornwallis*. But the ships were damaged too, and *Canopus* had a very narrow escape when a mine exploded just beyond her bow. No damage – but a good lesson in the terror that these waters definitely still held. The French came in to the Gulf of Xeros and shelled various defences without any particularly noticeable results. And that night the minesweepers were out again, trying to guard against another incident such as that which had befallen *Canopus*.

At noon on 3 March four British ships moved into the Straits and began duelling with Turkish field-guns. The Admiral could thank his stars, for the seaplanes flew and located the field batteries that were firing. The pilots and observers had begun to work out their communications problems with the ships. The art of war was being advanced.

The predictions of Winston Churchill of a week earlier seemed to be coming true, but with intense complications. The news that the British were working in a yeomanlike way to reduce the fortifications brought joy and terror. The Bulgarians were indeed re-thinking the whole question of loans and alliances. The Greek General Staff told the British military attaché that they could easily come into the war now and land four or five Greek divisions in the south of the peninsula. The Russians reported that they had changed their minds and could make an army corps available, as well as many ships of the Black Sea fleet. But the Russians did not want the Greeks involved and the Tsar felt strongly enough about the subject to tell the British Ambassador that it could not under any circumstances happen. Churchill had forgotten the old animosities and fears of the Mediterranean and the Black Sea; his desire to win the war against his country's enemies had blinded him to the reality of world politics. And it was world politics that came to the Turkish rescue now as much as any military force or generalship. The Greeks wanted a foothold on the Dardanelles, and the Russians were adamant that they should not have it. The days of Alexander the Macedonian were not forgotten in St Petersburg.

Under no conditions, Tsar Nicholas told King Constantine of Greece in a private message, would the Greek troops be allowed to enter Constantinople. The full import of that message was not lost on Churchill. What a war it would become if the Greeks fought the Russians and joined the

Germans! It was unthinkable – and the best that could be done with the situation was to lose those 250,000 Greek troops that might have been, that vital, immediate Greek support that could have carried the day for the Allies.

Military operations were now assuming a different pose. On 1 March General Birdwood began conferring with Admiral Wemyss, the base commander at Lemnos, and they talked about the forty thousand troops that might be coming from Egypt. It was all very vague. On 2 March the two commanders went over to Tenedos to confer with Admiral Carden and found him bemused by the problems posed by the mobile field-guns and the good use to which the Germans and Turks were putting them. Carden was concerned about the slowness with which the gun-knockout and minesweeping was going on. He told these officers that he was now of the opinion that the inner forts would have to be cleared away and these guns rendered quiet before they could get on with the minesweeping. And this meant troops. How many troops? On the scene, the necessities noted back in London were becoming imperatives.

4 March was a busy day at Tenedos and Lemnos. The seaplanes were out, but they were taking a pasting from Turks and German troops who seemed to have gained new heart. When one plane returned to the *Ark Royal*, its pilot counted twenty-eight bullet holes.

The Admiral ordered landing parties that day, to test his theory that more was needed in the way of men than he might readily offer at the moment. At Sedd-el-Bahr, 250 marines landed, and another 250 went ashore at Kum Kale, to find and silence those guns hidden in the hills. Carden took a strong interest: he put Admiral de Robeck and Brigadier General Trotman of the Birdwood force in direct charge – he wanted them to observe and see what they would be up against in the future. And he watched carefully himself from his bridge aboard *Inflexible*.

The results were much as he had feared they would be. The marines who assaulted Sedd-el-Bahr had rough going and did not get back to their ships until 3 pm with casualties. The marines who hit Kum Kale ran into serious opposition and did not manage to make any headway at all. It was going to take more force than the marines could then offer to silence those field pieces that could harry the minesweepers and destroyers and prevent the effective sweeping of the Straits. The success of the Germans and Turks in fighting the British brought more fury – for as the marines withdrew from Kum Kale, the enemy launched attacks, and the destroyers had to go in and cover to shell the trenches so that the Allied troops could get away. It was dark before the operation ended, and even then that was not the end. Two officers and nine men were left stranded on the shore, as darkness fell and the last boats got away. What was to be done? The answer came from a pair of destroyers. Lieutenant Commander A.B. Cunningham took in *Scorpion*, and Commander O.J. Prentis took in *Wolverine* – the pair of them ran dangerously close inshore, watching desperately for mines and enemy fire, and put whaleboats ashore under volunteers. They brought out five men and two officers. Still not all the men were out, and it took volunteers from the *Agamemnon* to pick up the last four men from the Kum Kale pier where they had been stranded.

Obviously, all was not going quite as placidly or successfully at the Dardanelles as the newspapers in London indicated these days. One had only to look at the casualty list from the day's operations: nineteen killed, twenty-three wounded and three men missing, plus some twenty sailors killed and wounded. Those figures gave Admiral Carden something to consider.

Back in London, Admiral Fisher was growing very restless at the slowness of the operation, the failure of the troops to appear or be in position to appear, and the general position of his adored fleet units. The more he considered the Dardanelles the less he liked it, and he warned Churchill that the Navy could send no more assistance to the area, not even a dinghy.

Lord Fisher was a very worried man.

15 'It Will Take Fourteen Days . . .'

Every day when the wireless and telegraph reports came in from the Dardanelles, the Admiralty War Group met to appreciate the situation, and Churchill asked his chief planner, Sir Henry Jackson, to sum it all up for them. From the early days of March, the results seemed highly satisfactory in a military way. Churchill telegraphed Admiral Carden and asked him just how long he thought it would take him to force the passage. On 2 March Carden had replied, 'It will take fourteen days . . .' – but that was before the attempt of 4 March to silence the small guns around the big forts. A few days later Admiral Carden would have some quite different thoughts on the subject. The failure of the marines had made him reconsider the problem.

On 5 March the *Queen Elizabeth* came into action again with those fifteen-inch guns. She, of course, was used very prudently, anchored west of Gallipoli in an area which had been well swept. The Turks knew of her presence there and had announced it to the world – the idea that Britain would send her newest and finest warship to the operation gave the Dardanelles a good deal of the importance it assumed in world thinking. The big battleship was in place in the morning, and at ten o'clock up came *Ark Royal* to offer the assistance of spotter planes for the gunners. Flight Lieutenant W.H.S.Garnett and Flight Commander Williamson were selected for the job and one of the Sopwiths was put over the side. The plane took off and began to climb after preliminary circling. The take-off was magnificent, the weather calm and the water almost glassy. No one could ask for more, and even as they climbed, they marvelled at it. The Sopwith climbed well, no turbulence disturbed the seaplane, and the pilot and observer looked ahead to the coast and the task they were to perform.

Suddenly, at three thousand feet, there came a smashing and a ripping sound. In a moment both men saw what had happened: the propeller of their plane had disintegrated under pressure, and they had no means of flight. The plane was not a good glider; it went into a tail spin, first flat and then growing tighter and uncontrollable. The plane spiralled down and crashed into the sea, where it was destroyed completely by the impact. Both men got out, both of them stunned, but they remained afloat until the boat of the destroyer *Usk* could come by and pick them out of the water. Garnett was only shaken, but Williamson was more severely hurt and was taken to the hospital ship for treatment. He was to be out of action for several weeks.

Back on the *Ark Royal* a second Sopwith was made ready and this time the propeller's laminations received more than usual scrutiny. Flight Lieutenant N.S.Douglas got aboard, along with Flight Sub-Lieutenant E.H.Dunning, and they took off just as easily as had the first Sopwith an hour before. Up went Douglas, pulling back on the stick, making long climbing turns to gain altitude and yet not overrun their objective, the peninsula ahead, where the *Queen Elizabeth* would throw her field of fire. In a few minutes they were in position. Dunning unpacked the wireless set that had been tinkered and manufactured into shape aboard the *Ark Royal* in those flightless days. He began tapping out a message and was delighted to have a response from *Queen Elizabeth*. They were ready to go – let the ship begin her fire.

Down below, amid the forts and lines of trenches, they could see little puffs of smoke as the enemy fired at them, but up in the blue the noise of the firing was nothing more than a little popping, like Chinese firecrackers. They were prepared for action.

Then, suddenly, the plane shuddered, and Dunning looked querulously at Douglas. He was hit, said the pilot. Where? In the leg. That meant they had to go home.

The Sopwith headed back for the *Ark Royal*, and the wounded pilot managed to land the plane safely. He was moved out into a boat, and Flight Lieutenant R.H.Kershaw took over the controls. But by this time precious hours had gone by, and when the pair of airmen arrived over the area of operations, Dunning had time only for a few messages and the ship time to send a few controlled shells before the light began to fail and the *Queen Elizabeth* moved out of range. Winston Churchill and Lord Fisher would have been upset to learn that the pride of the Royal Navy had been hit no fewer than seventeen times by the guns of the Turks as she stood offshore for her shelling chore. The damage was almost minimal – but the Turks were there trying every moment.

Worst of all, as the intelligence officers soon learned, all those shells she had poured into the forts and installations had been of little use. The Turks were moving their guns about, and they were learning every day how to do it more effectively. Admiral Carden had to put down the shooting of his favourite battleship that day as a total loss. Churchill's theory that big guns could destroy anything was simply not holding good here in the Dardanelles. One bit of good news did come in: Admiral Pierce of the East Indies Squadron arrived with his ships and began bombarding Smyrna. That *was* a break, but to Carden the big problem was still what was going to happen at the Dardanelles, for some of the assumptions on which the basic plan was made were now proving to be untrue. Luckily, from his point of view, the vanguard of the troops he might need had begun to arrive at Lemnos. A thousand Australians landed and went into camp, while another four thousand remained aboard their transports, waiting for camp facilities and water to be made available.

Commodore Keyes went aboard the *Queen Elizabeth* a day

or so after her action of 5 March and discovered the kind of damage the Turkish guns were capable of inflicting on the big battleship. She had lost some boats, and her superstructure had been pierced – mosquito harassment, no more. But the same kind of harassment occurred on 6 March when she went into action, and again the next day, and it was troublesome enough to prevent her from being an accurate weapon. She moved several times – the Turks or Germans were uncanny in being able to find her and range in on her with their six-inch guns. For two days she had very many narrow escapes from damage. Each day the battleships went after the forts, trench lines and gun positions. Each night the destroyers and minesweepers moved in to search out positions, in the strong glare of those German searchlights which were so very effective.

On 7 March the French went in – it was their turn to try for whatever glory was to be gained. *Lord Nelson* and *Agamemnon* fought with them until one o'clock in the afternoon when *Agamemnon* was hit by a fourteen-inch shell that put a sixteen-foot hole in her upper deck, wrecking the wardroom, and by another big shell that hit above the armour forward and knocked the men's waterclosets to pieces.

Lord Nelson was struck three feet below the waterline by a projectile which started rivets in her armour. Captain John McClintock was in the conning tower, and a splinter hit him in the head, while another wounded the Commander and a quartermaster.

The past week had marked a change in the Turkish attitude, first subtle and then vigorous. Late in February the landing parties of marines and the demolition experts had found it easy going. They had gone into the original forts and blown up the guns without much opposition. But the landing party on 4 March had come under heavy sniper fire and heavy direct opposition, in spite of hundreds of rounds of covering fire from the ships and heroic rescue efforts in the end. The fact was that the engagement was blown up by the

Turks in Constantinople into a tremendous Turkish victory against an attempted landing by the British. Morale rose sharply, and more confusion set in among the various elements of the Allied Command. General Birdwood certainly contributed to the confusion. After his visit to Carden, he telegraphed Lord Kitchener in London that he estimated the number of Turks in the vicinity of the Straits at forty thousand. He was not at all sure that the naval troops could force the Dardanelles, he said, but if they could, they would need the support of a major military expedition.

Now there was real disagreement as to what would be necessary to reach Constantinople. Churchill suggested that the forty thousand troops they had been talking about should be assembled and ready for landing at the Mudros base on Lemnos about 16 March. He thought that these troops would be enough to mop up after the fleet forced its way through piece after piece of the passage. Lord Kitchener seemed to agree and told Birdwood to prepare the troops for operations around Constantinople. But Birdwood had seen how difficult this mopping up was turning out to be. He had come just at the height of Carden's difficulties – and now he insisted that the taking of the forts and the progress of the fleet was going to be much slower than anyone seemed to expect. The men of the ships were beginning to agree; Commodore Keyes was making sure that Admiral Carden had the information about the difficulties they were facing, for new factors were constantly arising to be taken into account. For example, the minesweepers were basically unable to do their jobs at night, since they did not have the power to overcome the currents in the Straits when the tide was running.

On 8 March Admiral Carden came to see for himself in *Queen Elizabeth*. She entered the Straits and made three runs, firing eleven rounds against the fortifications at the Narrows. She made one spectacular hit. Seaplanes flew that day to try to help her, but the weather was so misty that they were unable to spot effectively, and the affair was not satisfactory;

at 3.30 the ships withdrew. That night again the trawlers failed to clear the minefields.

Admiral Carden had a hard night's thought. He had been engaged here for three weeks already, and he had estimated that four weeks was going to be necessary to clear the Straits. Aside from that first day's work, no real progress had been achieved, and each firing mission seemed to succeed less fully than the one before. When the planes did fly these days, they reported movements of troops and new fortifications going up. The resistance of the Turks had stiffened remarkably. The Kephez minefield that stood between him and the narrows was a serious obstacle.

Here was the point that had been considered in the original thinking on the Dardanelles operation, the point at which the resistance to the naval effort would be shown to be strong. Originally, all had agreed that at such a point as this the whole effort might be abandoned, and a landing made somewhere on the Mediterranean coast of the Turkish territory. Had Carden kept to the plan, and at this point said that the naval effort could not succeed, perhaps withdrawal would have been possible without much difficulty. And yet, in a propaganda sense, it would have already been disastrous. The newspapers of the world had blown up the British effort to enormous proportions. The Turks were fully alerted, and the slow nature of the British effort had given them new hope. Admiral Pierce was besieging Smyrna with considerable success – new pressures were mounting every day.

9 March was another terrible day, with low visibility of the kind that had continually hammered Admiral Carden and was sapping his personal resistance all the time. He was drawn and haggard, an ill man in a dreadful situation that had progressed beyond his control. By day the battleships moved in and fired, and by night they withdrew while the Turks repaired the damages and the little trawlers tried to clear the Kephez minefields that stood between the battleships and the Narrows. The next day was nearly as bad: the

ships operated but not effectually. That night seven mine-sweepers went in with picket boats and explosive sweeps – a truly desperate attempt. One trawler was lost. The attempt failed.

Admiral Carden was in touch with London every day, and there rumours and ideas chased one another through the meetings and across the thousands of pages of reports and memoranda that helpful souls created. Churchill was flushed and jumpy, as all who knew him well quite expected ('I know how restless and impatient W.C. must be,' wrote Commodore Keyes from the Dardanelles at this juncture). But there was not the slightest thought in Churchill's mind that the failure he had once foreseen so casually was at hand. On the 4th he was supremely confident. The army had simply got to get cracking, he wrote to Kitchener, for naval operations at the Dardanelles could not be delayed waiting for troops to come up, 'as we must get into the Marmara as soon as possible in the normal course'.

A careful reader of messages could sense the change in Carden's attitude in the difficulties and failures of the past few days. That first phase of the bombardment had seemed so easy, but the combination of events and weather had made the second phase almost hellish in its promise and delay. On 9 March Carden showed his anxiety by telling the Admiralty that he could do no more under present circumstances until his air service was reinforced. The seaplanes of *Ark Royal* were not able to give him what he needed. That was London's problem. In the interim he would concentrate on clearing the minefield. Sir Henry Jackson was a wise old bird, and when he began adding up the indeterminates in the messages, he came to the conclusion that Carden's situation indicated that it was time for the landing of troops. The light guns on the hillsides must be silenced, and the best way he could think was to land forces on the Gallipoli peninsula, the European side which was basically deserted, and thus from the heights command the Asian side with field guns.

Next day, 10 March, at the War Council meeting, Lord Kitchener reversed his decision on the subject of the regulars of the 29th Division. Obviously Winston Churchill's barrage of messages, and the constant pressure to which he had subjected the War Office, was paying off here. But of course, in a way Churchill was supported by the troops in the field – General Birdwood, who had been on the scene, felt very strongly that a sizeable military force must be committed. Whatever the cause, Kitchener now announced that he was willing to put 130,000 men against the Turkish armies in order to take the Dardanelles. Quite a change from an operation that had begun as a sort of diversionary military exercise to help out a southern Russian army under siege.

16   The Fatal Commitment

At the War Council meeting on 10 March, Winston Churchill was for once left nearly speechless. He was terribly upset by the political turn events had taken in the Balkans, particularly by the strange attitude of the Russians which threatened to turn the war upside down. He had observed events since 3 March and saw that Carden's progress was slowing to a halt. He also learned, with some surprise, that the Turks were turning out to be much tougher than anyone had suspected. Imagine: in the attack of 6 March the old Turkish battleship *Barbarossa* had opened fire on *Queen Elizabeth* from her anchorage inside the Straits off Maidos. Those ancient eleven-inch guns did not hit the *Queen*, but they cheered the Turks immensely and gave indication of the difficulties in which the Allies had immersed themselves. Churchill was equipped at this meeting with a mountain of statistics. They told how many times each fort had been hit, how many guns had been blown up, how many shells had been expended and how few were the casualties. He observed that he thought the Navy could still win through on the original plan, but he was certainly glad to hear that the troops would be available if they were required. By now, Lord Kitchener was certain that the troops were required, and he was in motion to put them ashore on the Gallipoli peninsula.

Having decided, Kitchener moved. He appointed Sir Ian Hamilton as commander of the force on 12 March. Churchill suggested that Hamilton should leave the same afternoon, but it was Friday 13 March before he crossed over from Dover in a warship, took a special train across France with his staff of thirteen, and embarked on a thirty-knot cruiser at Marseilles for Mudros. The British could act when they had to, and Hamilton reached his destination on 17 March.

At the meeting of the War Council on 10 March it was apparent that Admiral Carden was a dispirited man. Next day it was apparent everywhere that naval operations at the Dardanelles were at a standstill, the British ships stymied by the minefield and those manoeuvrable field-guns up in the hills that would not get knocked out and stay knocked out.

So Winston Churchill pressed for action. No longer was there the slightest indication that the operation might be abandoned. Instead, a message was sent to Carden urging him to take greater risks, including that of the loss of ships. The Admiralty wanted that minefield forced and those forts at the Narrows overwhelmed, and they wanted it done in a hurry. The message that went out from London to Carden on the night of 11 March made that all very clear.

On 12 March Carden could have wrung his hands. Once again the day dawned grey and leaden. How could he meet London's demands in weather like this? The battleships had no help from the air. The trawlers could not fight the currents any better than before. Another day of irritation. In exasperation, Carden ordered a major sweeping effort on the night of 13 March, against a current that sometimes ran at four knots. At first the battleships laid down a barrage on the positions of the guns – thus thoroughly alerting the Turks and Germans to a night action.

The defenders ashore had learned a good deal in the last few weeks. They waited out the bombardment and watched through their night glasses as seven sweepers and five picket boats came in through the narrow strait towards the mine-fields. Once in a while, as if to encourage the British by the weakness of their response, a gun ashore would fire a single round.

The ships moved in. The Turks let them get right into the middle of the minefield. Then all the searchlights in the area suddenly went out at a signal. They had been idly switching the water as a cow switches her tail against flies. The lights stayed out for a full minute, then they came on, concentrated on the Allied flotilla. The British just then learned that the Turks and Germans had also concentrated sixty or seventy guns against them, and they were firing from both sides of the Straits.

The deadly fire cut the wires of the sweeps and the winches that ran them, and the trawlers began to take shells that would bounce off the armoured decks of the *Queen Elizabeth* but which smashed wood in these little boats. Soon five of the sweepers were in real trouble, and the other two were barely able to get their sweeps out. The Turks were throwing everything they had at the British – from six-inch shells to shrapnel and rifle fire. Some strings of mines were detached, some mines were exploded, but the damage was far worse to the attackers than to the defenders. One trawler took eighty-four gun hits – luckily without a casualty. When the operation ended, *Amethyst* was badly damaged and four of the trawlers were out of operation.

So the admirals on the scene came to a new conclusion: they could not clear the minefield at night. Carden then knew what he had to do in view of the kind of messages and encouragement he was getting from London. He had to put on the 'big Push' – a sledgehammer blow at the defences of the Narrows. The Admiral knew after that night's work that it was going to be costly, how costly London might not yet understand, but he and the other senior officers also knew their Churchill and what was demanded of them here. It was no work for a sick man. And Carden was sick, even his senior officers knew it, although they did not suspect that he was more than 'seedy'.

Admiral Carden was a courageous and able officer. After the discouragement of the unlucky night of Friday, 13 March, he had 'shot the wad' of half-measures. He sent a plucky message to London, concurring in the need for strong and swift action. But he warned London that his losses might indeed be great, that the Admiralty should hold new and powerful ships in readiness for the call on short notice and that plenty of ammunition should be sent on immediately. Also, he now wanted the troops to be ready to move immediately to ensure the lines of communications, once he had forced the Narrows and entered the Sea of Marmara.

No question that he could do it. No question about the cost in lives and ammunition. It was necessary and, in the best British naval tradition, that is how it was to be.

Saturday was a busy day in London. The commitment of troops was growing, and Churchill put pressure on Admiral Carden to speed his operation. Carden agreed. He told London that he would drive home the attack against the Narrows and enter the Sea of Marmara as soon as the weather permitted. He was committed to a major action of his naval forces, and he knew it. But his problem then became very personal. Could he, sick and tired as he was, manage such an operation? Carden did not believe he could, and so he had a long conversation with Admiral de Robeck, and then ordered his servants to pack up his belongings and move them from flagship *Inflexible* over to the *Blenheim*. He was too ill to command.

De Robeck had argued gamely that Carden ought to retain command, exercising his authority through Keyes if necessary and simply lying low until he felt better. Carden agreed in that last conversation that he would think about it, but his honour as an officer would not let him lie sick, and yet take credit for the glory that might come to the fleet. Making the decision, Carden ordered his flag lieutenant to send out a general signal saying that he was going on the sick-list, and command was handed to Admiral de Robeck. Then Carden called in Keyes and made it official by handing over a letter to be sent to de Robeck's ship.

Keyes was a persuasive character. He argued that the Admiral's indisposition was only from the day's luncheon ('that beastly suet and treacle pudding'), and he persuaded Carden to delay. It was too late, said the Admiral. Not at all, said Keyes. The Admiral would find that none of his orders had been carried out. Carden promised to see the doctors on board the hospital ship as soon as possible and to wait until their consultation before taking such drastic action.

There was good reason for Keyes and de Robeck to want to keep their Admiral in the game. The plan was set, the organization was functioning. De Robeck was not the next senior officer in the area: he was outranked by Admiral Pierce who was bombarding Smyrna and by Admiral Wemyss who was commanding the base. To try on the eve of an operation to put a new commander in charge of a delicate problem was a most risky business, and one not relished by the professionals who had been spending a month at this task already.

But on 16 March the ship's doctor of *Inflexible* ('a regular mugwump') brought the matter up again. He could not take responsibility for the Admiral's health unless Carden had complete rest, he said. De Robeck and Keyes pointed out that to relinquish command on the eve of an important operation was professional suicide. If Carden quitted now, no matter what the justification, he was finished. They so bullied the doctor that he returned to the Admiral and said that if he would keep quiet for a few days, he might be all right. They argued. The Admiral issued his orders again, but soon Keyes refused to obey them and won another round when he declared that he had no confidence in the 'mugwump' and wanted the Admiral to see the chief surgeon of the hospital ship *Soudan* next day. The surgeon was a volunteer, a Harley Street specialist, and he ought to know what he was talking about.

A medical board assembled. They thumped the Admiral and looked at his records and conferred with dignity in secrecy. Then they returned to the officers to say that the Admiral was indeed sick: he was suffering from nervous collapse and would have a complete breakdown if he did not take two or three weeks off and stay in bed. Complete rest, that was the indicated treatment.

There might have been a dreadful problem had the wrong man been chosen to lead the operation, but Carden sent a secret message to Churchill recommending Rear-Admiral de Robeck, and Churchill was wise enough to understand and give de Robeck a temporary appointment as Vice-Admiral, which made him senior officer. Churchill did this in spite of the fact that he had quarrelled with de Robeck earlier, and de Robeck regarded himself as being on the minister's black list.

On 17 March Churchill sent a tactful message to de Robeck inquiring whether he agreed with the plans ('If not, do not hesitate to say so'), appointing Wemyss as second-in-command officially, which settled all lines of succession, and urging action and quick co-operation with General Hamilton.

That hurried man no sooner arrived in the area on 17 March than he was hustled off to a meeting aboard *Queen Elizabeth* in which de Robeck reviewed all that had gone before, assessed his commanders and tried to familiarize himself with everything that was going on in the whole theatre of operation. The politicians were out of it now. Even the Admiralty in London had done all that deskbound admirals could do. The Navy was committed to rushing the forts that guarded the minefields before the Narrows.

The conference agreed that this was indeed the case and that the sooner the better. The French were there; the military were there; the admirals were in attendance and so were the marines. All was settled.

The next morning, Admiral de Robeck's staff were up early, scanning the dawn skies and checking the wind. Not long after sun-up, the Admiral sent a message: weather fine; operations about to begin. And then there was silence from the fleet assembled at the Dardanelles.

London and the world must wait.

17   The Attack

Admiral de Robeck had aired certain fears at the meeting of high officers aboard the *Queen Elizabeth* the day before. He was particularly concerned about the clever manner in which the Turks and Germans were making use of the mobile artillery in the hills and crannies behind the forts. The ships could silence the big guns that were in place, but those movable ones. . . . Those guns could not seriously damage the fleet, everyone agreed, but they could make a really heroic job for the minesweepers, because they had sunk sweepers before. De Robeck would have liked very much to have real naval minesweepers for the task, but that was impossible. The problem nagged, but there was nothing that could be done about it. He was worried about the mines and he would continue to worry about them. He was also committed.

All night long the minesweepers had been out in the current, struggling under the watchful eyes of four destroyers. They had not accomplished much, and no one really expected them to do so, but they had kept moving and kept working and had cleared away a little patch of mines.

At six o'clock in the morning, just after the Admiral sent his telegram about the beginning of operations, the destroyer *Mosquito* sank three mines in Morto Bay, not far from the entrance to the Straits on the European side. Two and a half hours later the area was reported clear, and at 10.30 came the signal 'ready for action'.

The ships of the fleet split up. Ten battleships were assigned to the attack, and six were assigned to relieve them at four-hour intervals. The four most modern ships were to start off,

Senior?

156

sitting in the protected waters and firing at the forts on the other side of the minefields, about eight miles away. These ships were *Queen Elizabeth*, *Agamemnon*, *Lord Nelson* and *Inflexible*. Two other ships were to fire at closer defences around the minefield. They were designated Line A. Line B consisted of the four French vessels previously mentioned, *Cornwall* and *Canopus* that would cover the minesweepers during the night, and six old battleships that would work in relief.

The idea was that the battleships would move piecemeal, opening up on fortifications, destroying them and then waiting while the minesweepers did their work unobstructed and going on a few thousand more yards. It was a sort of pick-a-back plan, based on the power of powder, shot and shell over rock, dirt and fixed gun installations.

Ten days earlier the bombarding area had been free of mines, and ever since that time the minesweepers had been sweeping. The British had the feeling that the area was clear. Just to make sure, a picket boat was assigned to every battleship to destroy any mines that could be found.

The ships went to work against the guns on the Asian side at eleven o'clock, and everything seemed to be going very well. *Queen Elizabeth* was firing effectively – after one shot a huge explosion was noted in a fort well along the route. Other ships were firing on the six-inch guns, and the six-inch guns ashore were firing back. Their fire was annoying to some of the vessels but no more than that at this stage of the battle. The British were moving right along.

Just after noon Line B moved into action. The British vessels were now coming close to danger. For what they did not know was that ten days earlier the little Turkish steamer *Nousret* had sneaked out in the depth of a squally night, while the British destroyers were withdrawing, and had laid a new line of twenty mines in Eren Keui Bay, parallel to the shore, about a hundred yards apart – another little example of the effect that delay and waste of time had upon the morale of the Turks. They were making many diversions and extending their activity; the early hours of dispirited behaviour were long behind them. It showed in the firing that day.

Commodore Keyes was in the conning tower of the *Queen Elizabeth,* and he noticed the difference. He attributed it all to German gunners, which was not quite the case. But everyone could see that the enemy was making the utmost use of the six-inch guns that kept appearing in the hills on both sides. The guns fired against the big ships in salvoes, dropping three shells in a salvo. There was no point in trying a flat trajectory against armoured vessels, so they fired high, lobbing the shells into the air so they would fall as nearly straight down as possible and create utmost damage.

One shell hit the wireless rigging of the *Queen Elizabeth* and knocked it out for a time. That same burst sent dust and dirt into the conning-tower slits and nearly blinded Commodore Keyes. Across the Strait the same was happening to *Inflexible.* Her bridge caught fire and blazed away. A shell hit the fore control top, killing or wounding everyone there, and the fires were blazing so brilliantly that the ship had to move and get before the wind in order to control it. At just about the same time, *Inflexible*'s picket boat was struck squarely and sunk. Those Germans and Turks with their six-inch guns were firing like heroes. At 1.15 *Suffren* was hit several times. *Lord Nelson* was straddled by a six-inch battery.

All this action was happening at once, about two hours after the commencement of the battle. The British advance was very definitely slowed; the ships sent up grey streams of cordite smoke, and the forts lay under a pall of smoke created by their own firing and the hits of the battleship shells.

At noon one of the Wight seaplanes took to the air, to discover the progress of the ships' firing. They reported that four of the forts were manned and firing as rapidly as the guns could be worked. No easy pickings here. What they did not know, and what they did not see, was *another* sowing of mines that had been laid the night before by Turks and Germans in small craft, going out to brave the dangers of the enemy fleet.

The Wight reported what it could, and then came back to shore, and a Sopwith went up, to say very soon that most of the forts had stopped firing. (The Turks had indeed slowed down, to clear and clean their guns from the dirt and grit that was falling all around them in the many hits on the fortifications made by the British naval guns.)

Led by Admiral Guepratte, the French were out-doing themselves in their rate of fire and the daring with which they moved in close to the forts to hit at them. Those present watched in awe at the scene of might and magnificence that unfolded before them – the big, majestic ships wheeling and firing as they moved, and the forts firing back – the sea alive with splashes and even smashed vessels, men bleeding and dying in the forts and on the decks of ships. Looking down from on high, the gods of war would have been bemused.

The hour between one and two o'clock in the afternoon was the crucial period. At Fort 13 a tremendous explosion rocked the works, and the fort went silent. Noticeably, the Turkish forts slackened in their placement of the hail of death, and one might have thought that they had been knocked out or were running short of ammunition. The French were punishing two forts severely, and it was noticeable. Soon there was no return of fire. By quarter to two the fire from all the forts had nearly ceased, and, noting this from his command position, Admiral de Robeck ordered the inner line to come out, so that an appraisal of the effort could be made, the ships could regroup, the mines could be swept and the force could move onwards through the Straits as the plan called for the ships to do. The Narrows did not seem far away, and beyond them lay the prize of the Sea of Marmara.

Bravely, the sea tugging at their bows, the French vessels led the way out, *Suffren* in the fore with *Bouvet* following immediately behind her. *Suffren* came right along. Then as *Bouvet* turned, Admiral de Robeck could see from his bridge a large explosion on the starboard side of the vessel, abaft the after bridge. And with the explosion came fire and haze, haloed in black smoke that curled up thickly. The fires grew denser, and the smoke rose higher. The ship trembled and lost way, and men began scrambling about her decks. More explosions began to shoot fire and smoke upwards. It was apparent to the Admiral that the ship had been badly struck and was deep in trouble. The fires burned, the damage control parties could not stifle them, and then, a moment later, another explosion occurred, and *Bouvet* swung over to her starboard side, trembled and turned, to capsize and sink before the startled eyes of the assembled fleet.

This was indeed Turkish vengeance for the sinking of the *Messudiyeh* a few short weeks ago. It was obvious that *Bouvet* had struck a mine or mines, but it was not obvious that the Allied ships were moving into a new minefield. That, alas, was the net of their latest action, and the bravery of the French in particular had carried them inshore into waters that were supposedly cleared – waters that had been cleared as recently as the night before. *Suffren* stood by the anxious flagship, waiting and helping as she could until all the survivors were picked up. But there were few – only sixty-six men of the hundreds who had been aboard the ship.

By 2.15 the action was coming to an end for the moment. *Queen Elizabeth* and *Lord Nelson* were the only ships still firing, and on shore the Turkish forts were quiet, though Turkish troops were gathering near Kephez point, making ready to repel the invasion which the Turks and Germans expected to accompany the movement of the battleships up the Strait. But that movement was in doubt. The sinking of *Bouvet* was a distinct shock. Also, there was some question in the minds of the Allied officers as to just how *Bouvet* had met her end. Aboard *Queen Elizabeth* it seemed that she had taken a heavy calibre shell. Some of the French thought that she had suffered an internal explosion, caused perhaps by smouldering fires aft from a six-inch hit, and that her magazines had gone up. The fact was that she was just over and into the new minefield. But the confusion as to how she had gone down made it a harder task for Admiral de Robeck to consider his next action.

De Robeck watched and waited. He was proceeding according to plan. About twenty minutes later, the reserve line of six battleships passed by the others and moved in to engage the forts. Only one Turkish fort was sending up any shells at all at the time, and they concentrated on it. Suddenly there was an explosion against the side of *Irresistible*, and that caused the forts to start firing furiously on her. *Queen Elizabeth* took aim on Fort 19, the most aggressive of them, and began firing salvoes. In a few moments that fort shut down its guns. The firing continued until 4.11, the ships working over the fortifications but not stopping the Turkish return fire. At that moment, *Inflexible*, the old flagship, hit a mine – just as Admiral de Robeck was noting with considerable satisfaction that the personnel of the forts seemed to be fleeing.

It was the critical moment of the battle. The Allies did not know it but the Turks were short of ammunition. *Irresistible* had broken down and appeared to be dead in the water. She was listing noticeably, which meant serious trouble aboard. The Admiral sent the destroyer *Wear* to discover the trouble, after he was unable to raise her on the wireless and could make no sense of visual signals. *Wear* came back in half an hour, carrying twenty-two officers and nearly six hundred crewmen whom she had taken off. *Irresistible* was indeed in trouble: she had struck a mine, not just come up alongside one, and both her engine rooms had flooded out and she was unable to continue the battle. The captain had stayed aboard, keeping the executive officer and ten volunteers and was hoping for a tow.

Ocean was now detailed to try to help *Irresistible*. She proceeded to the Asian shore but found that *Irresistible* was in too close, listing badly at right angles to the shore, and she could not pass around her to get at the right angle to the current so as to make a tow possible. The Admiral then ordered that *Irresistible* be left where she was, under the skeleton crew, until dark. Then, under cover of night and silence, an attempt would be made to take her off. Meanwhile she would be watched, and if there was danger of her going aground, a destroyer would torpedo and sink the ship in deep water.

This manœuvring and consideration took a long time, and it was six o'clock in the evening before *Ocean* was able to withdraw to join the other ships. At 6.05, not far from where she had left *Irresistible*, *Ocean* struck another of the mines laid the night before and immediately began to list to starboard about fifteen degrees. The jubilant Turks opened fire, and one well-placed shot struck the steering mechanism on the starboard side, aft, and jammed the helm almost hard aport.

Now *Ocean* had to slow to a stop, and her list grew greater. Soon the Captain decided to disembark the crew, who were put into destroyers that came alongside under fire to take the men off. The Captain of the *Ocean* went off, too, into a destroyer, but an hour or so later he returned to his ship and checked to see that no one was left aboard. Then, around 7.30 that night, the *Ocean* was abandoned in the middle of the Dardanelles Straits.

Later that night officers of *Irresistible* and *Ocean* came back in a flotilla of destroyers and minesweepers, with the thought of towing the two vessels to safety. By that time both ships had sunk. Sadly enough, those who had watched reported that *Irresistible* had drifted in to the range of the Narrows forts, which were alert and vigorous that night and used up much of their remaining ammunition on the battleship until she went down.

As for the other ships, many of them had taken damage that they did not expect from the guns of the Turks. *Inflexible* reached Tenedos and safety, and so did *Gaulois* and *Suffren*, and all three ships were sent back to Malta for major repairs.

But the real damage was to the British plan, for, if the Admiral and his officers had but known it, by forging onwards that day after *Irresistible* was hit, they could have forced the Straits. So much seems quite sure in hindsight.

At two o'clock in the afternoon, when the critical moment

The Attack

came, the Turks were in very poor condition. The two major forts in the narrows, Chanak Kale on the Asian side and Kilid Bahr on the European, were under fire then; their telephonic communication was out and they were out of touch with the world; many of the guns were destroyed, and some were unable to fire because the shells from the big battleships had covered them with earth.

It was not a question of thousands of dead or even hundreds – that was the whole secret of the Dardanelles operation that Winston Churchill had guessed from the opening days. At these major bastions of defence the dead were four officers and forty men. In the whole action the Turks lost only 150 men, and the British lost only sixty-one men. The French, unlucky in the explosion of *Bouvet*, suffered six hundred casualties – out of all proportion to the battle waged. The naval battle of the Dardanelles was never a question of huge forces pitted against one another. It was a question of naval ships pitted against shore defences, with the full belief of Churchill and some others that the naval forces could win their way through the Narrows.

But it did not happen. Ambassador Morgenthau in Constantinople said that, had the British pressed through, they would certainly have won (in spite of those mines still to be passed). German gunners who had been at Chanak had expected the British to win through, either that day or the next. They could not hold out much longer, and they expected hourly to see the line of grey ships thread its way into the Sea of Marmara. Enver Pasha himself said that if the British had pressed on, willing to lose ships as British commanders had always been willing to sacrifice for victory, then the victory would have been de Robeck's, and the control of the Dardanelles would have been won.

But it would have taken a Nelson to do the job, and there was no Nelson afloat at the point where the narrows of the Dardanelles meets the width of the Aegean. That was the disaster of the Dardanelles.

18   Aftermath

The attack on the Dardanelles had promised so much to the Allied cause and had grown to demand much attention from the whole world. But its aftermath was first anti-climax, then very nearly comic opera and finally real tragedy and the loss of thousands of lives, on the principle that brute strength could win out where audacity had failed. But it was not audacity that failed. It was men who failed audacity. For they took too much time in thinking rather than acting. The small, swift, desperate operation envisaged by Churchill and some others, followed by the rapid movement of troops on to the European shore of the Gallipoli peninsula, would have assured control of the Dardanelles, even if the Turkish government had not fallen, as many observers on the scene expected. But action was forsaken for information and study that night.

Admiral de Robeck broke off the battle with darkness, with the apparent intention of resuming the fighting in the morning. The squadron was ready for action next day. But London equivocated: the War Council met on 19 March and said that de Robeck could continue the operation 'if he saw fit'. On the 20th de Robeck planned, changing the usage of his forces and apparently still determined to go ahead. There seemed little reason for not doing so – the situation of the Turks was not radically altered; they were not heavily resupplied nor had their gun situation improved. The troops, with their German leaders and Turkish officers, fully expected a breakthrough and the loss of the area.

But on 22 March caution intervened. De Robeck called a meeting of admirals and generals aboard the *Queen Elizabeth*.

There, the chemistry of the Dardanelles operation underwent a change. Out of that meeting came a message to London to the effect that the Dardanelles operation must have troops, that it could not succeed without them. The question was of emphasis. Bringing up the troops on hand at Mudros was one thing, but waiting for the hundreds of thousands in the division was something else. When the generals started thinking, they thought in terms of armies – and that kind of thinking dominated the day aboard the splendid new battleship, which symbolized a quite different warfare.

In London, the news brought about a crisis that reopened old wounds. Winston Churchill and the Prime Minister were all for going ahead and forcing the Dardanelles with the ships. Churchill drafted just such a message. It was resisted by Admirals Fisher and Jackson, on the old command principle that the man on the spot knew more than the politicians in Whitehall.

And what politician dared face such unanimity and take the possible consequences of a ruined career if he was wrong – when he could not have the picture clear in his mind? Churchill and the other politicians backed down. They asked questions, but they backed down.

'What has happened since the 21st to make you alter your intention . . .?' asked the First Lord plaintively. The reply, when it came, was military gobbledegook: '. . . conferred with General and heard his proposals . . . co-operation of army and navy was considered by him a sound operation of war . . . fully prepared to work with the navy . . . *etcetera, etcetera*'. The General, having been brought into the operation, had already begun making his own plans for the kind of military manœuvre a general would make.

And there was the tragedy. The ships settled down to wait for the troops. More and bigger of everything was wanted. More and bigger came. It became Kitchener's operation and an army show. The delay and the build-up of Allied troops gave the Turks time to prepare, and the failure to win through gave the Turks courage and the feeling that they had scored a great victory with a handful of men, which, if one looks at it from the Turkish point of view, they most certainly had done. They had outfaced the Royal Navy.

In the dreadful carnage and error and bad luck that followed, the British forces were decimated, and the men from 'down under' took the brunt of it. So grave was the disaster of Gallipoli that it brought down the government and wrecked many a notable career at home as well as in the field. Winston Churchill's political position was injured, and he took years to recover.

Does that mean that the Dardanelles should never have been essayed as a naval breakthrough? Perhaps, given the nature of the warfare that developed after 1914. But then again – in 1940 in France, later on Crete, at Midway, at Dienbienphu, it was the audacious that turned the tides in military as well as naval warfare. So validity of the study of the naval attempt to break through the Dardanelles is that story of the small and the large. The men who were on the scene were brave and self-sacrificing, ready for death and looking for glory, from submariner to intrepid aviator, from stoker to brave marine. There were stories to be told, such as those of *B-11* and the sinking of *Bouvet*. There were brave battle tales from nearly every action of the war.

But at the Dardanelles the real story was the story of audacity, how it succeeded on the lower levels when men were able to force their way into action, and how it failed when an admiral put himself in the hands of a committee.